Maria Edgeworth

Twayne's English Authors Series

Herbert Sussman, Editor
Northeastern University

TEAS 375

MARIA EDGEWORTH
From a portrait of
the Edgeworth family, 1787,
by Adam Buck

Maria Edgeworth

By Elizabeth Harden

Wright State University

Twayne Publishers • *Boston*

Maria Edgeworth

Elizabeth Harden

Copyright © 1984 by G. K. Hall & Company
All Rights Reserved
Published by Twayne Publishers
A Division of G. K. Hall & Company
70 Lincoln Street
Boston, Massachusetts 02111

Book Production by Marne B. Sultz

Book Design by Barbara Anderson

Printed on permanent/durable acid-free
paper and bound in the United States of America.

**Library of Congress Cataloging in
Publication Data.**

Harden, O. Elizabeth McWhorter (Oleta Elizabeth
    McWhorter), 1935-
    Maria Edgeworth.

    (Twayne's English authors series; TEAS 375)
    Bibliography: p. 136
    Includes index.
    1. Edgeworth, Maria, 1767–1849
—Criticism and interpretation.
I. Title.   II. Series.
PR4647.H26   1984   823'.7   84–8571
ISBN 0–8057–6879–3

Contents

About the Author

Elizabeth Harden, a native of Kentucky, received her B.A. in English from Western Kentucky University and her M.A. and Ph.D. degrees in English from the University of Arkansas. She is currently professor of English at Wright State University. A member of the faculty there since 1966, she has held executive administrative posts in addition to full-time teaching. Following the publication of her first book, *Maria Edgeworth's Art of Prose Fiction,* she researched Edgeworth material in Ireland and England. Her major teaching and research interests are Anglo-Irish literature, English romanticism, and the nineteenth-century British novel. She is currently working on another book on nineteenth-century Irish novelists.

Preface

Maria Edgeworth's literary reputation in this century has suffered from neglect and misreading. Most critics and historians of the novel have tended to accept clichés about her influence on Scott and her dependence on her father and then assign her to oblivion. Yet it is obvious that Christina Colvin's two valuable editions of Edgeworth family letters and Marilyn Butler's definitive biography (both published in the 1970s) have begun to revolutionize Edgeworth scholarship, as evidenced by recent doctoral theses and scholarly articles.

My earlier study of Maria Edgeworth was an attempt to examine the techniques of her fiction from a modern critical perspective. In the decade since that book was published, my thinking about her fiction has altered. As the result of recent scholarship, I have come to see that her reputation as one of the most important and influential fiction writers of her time was fully deserved. The opportunity to examine an important collection of the unpublished family letters has made me more fully aware of the influences that shaped her career. But most important, a detailed rereading of her fiction has convinced me that she is a gifted writer and an original thinker whose power has not been sufficiently recognized in this century.

My aim in the present study is to demonstrate that many of Maria Edgeworth's works still have valid claims on our attention. And because her father and family were the most important influences on her career, I have devoted the opening chapter to biographical detail to help the reader understand the conditions under which she worked and by which her intentions were shaped. The chapters that follow attempt to encompass the total body of her work and are arranged, not chronologically, but according to the audiences to which the works are addressed: children, adolescents, and adults. The Irish novels have been grouped in one chapter since they, too, were designed for a specific audience. I have not, of course, tried to discuss each of the children's stories, tales, or fugitive pieces. But I have included all of the major novels and have selected works for children and adolescents which are perhaps best representative of the fiction for these age groups.

Throughout the book, I have, to some extent, followed traditional analysis of such matters as characterization, plot, and theme. I have tried to see each work individually as a product of its time and its author's purpose; but I have also attempted to suggest what is valuable, unique, and original. Several of the readings, I realize, are entirely my own. And behind them and the modest plan and arrangement of this book lurks a shamefully selfish hope: that others will read and reread Maria Edgeworth and will hopefully find reason to join in a common effort to rescue her—at least, partially—from the undeserved oblivion into which she has fallen.

In writing this book, I have incurred a number of personal debts that I am happy to acknowledge. I am particularly indebted to Christina Colvin, who not only supplied me with information about Edgeworth family history, but also permitted me to review family papers and letters on loan to her at the Bodleian Library, Oxford. To E. J. S. Parsons, secretary and deputy librarian, and to members of the Bodleian Library staff, I am most grateful for helpful professional assistance while I was there. I also wish to thank Ailfrid Mac-Lochlainn, former director of the National Library of Ireland, and Marian Keaney, county librarian for the Longford-Westmeath County Library, for permission to examine their Edgeworth collections. To Sister Winnifred and the staff of Edgeworthstown Nursing Home, and to Mr. Gogan and Mrs. Lynch of Edgeworthstown, Ireland, I am grateful for warm memories of two visits during which they shared with me many interesting details about the original Edgeworth family dwelling, the family church and cemetery, and the Edgeworth museum.

Some fifteen libraries generously lent materials during the progress of my study, and I express thanks to them and to Joy Iddings, who processed my interlibrary loans with courtesy and dispatch. To Wright State University and to the College of Liberal Arts, I owe deep thanks for a year's sabbatical and for a travel grant that helped make possible the earlier stages of research. Thanks of a more personal nature are due to my friend and colleague, Peter Bracher, who read the manuscript, helped me with valuable suggestions, and offered me kind encouragement throughout the study. I owe a profound debt of thanks to Eileen Sestito and Carol Chandler for preparing the manuscript. But perhaps I owe most to my husband

Dennis, who gave me up to countless hours of work and whose affectionate and remarkably durable support made the whole project seem worthwhile.

Elizabeth Harden

Wright State University

Chronology

1768 Maria Edgeworth born on 1 January at Black Bourton, Oxon, third child of Richard Lovell Edgeworth.

1773 March, mother dies. 17 July, father marries Honora Sneyd. Edgeworths lived in Ireland at Edgeworthstown until early 1776.

1775–1780 Attends Mrs. Latuffiere's school at Derby.

1780 1 May, Honora Edgeworth dies. 25 December, father marries Elizabeth Sneyd in London.

1781 Attends Mrs. Devis's school in Upper Wimpole Street, London. Spends some holidays at home of Thomas Day.

1782 June, Edgeworths return to Ireland to live at Edgeworthstown. Irish independency established.

1783 *Adèle et Théodore* (Maria's translation of Madame de Genlis; printed but withdrawn before publication).

1791–1793 Two-year residence in England.

1795 *Letters for Literary Ladies,* partly epistolary.

1796 *The Parent's Assistant,* a collection of children's stories.

1797 November, father's third wife dies.

1798 31 May, father marries Frances Anne Beaufort. *Practical Education,* a handbook for educating children, by Maria and her father.

1799 April, visits England; September, returns to Ireland.

1800 *Castle Rackrent,* first novel, published anonymously. Union of Great Britain and Ireland.

1801 *Early Lessons, Moral Tales, Belinda,* and *The Mental Thermometer.*

1802 *Essay on Irish Bulls,* with father.

1802–1803 Visits England, France, and Scotland. Receives marriage proposal from A. N. C. Edelcrantz, a Swedish Count.

1804 *Popular Tales.*

1805 *The Modern Griselda.*

1806 *Leonora,* only epistolary novel.

1807 Reviews John Carr's "The Stranger in Ireland," with father.

1809 *Essays on Professional Education* and *Tales of Fashionable Life,* first series.

1811 Preface and notes to *Cottage Dialogues Among the Irish Peasantry,* by Mary Leadbeater.

1812 *Tales of Fashionable Life,* second series.

1813 Visits England. Meets Byron in London. Lionized as authoress.

1814 *Patronage. Continuation of Early Lessons,* with father.

1816 *Readings on Poetry,* with father.

1817 June, father dies. *Harrington, Ormond,* and *Comic Dramas.*

1818 Visits England.

1820 *Memoirs of Richard Lovell Edgeworth,* by Maria and father. Visits England, France, and Switzerland.

1821 *Rosamond: A Sequel to Early Lessons.* Visits England.

1822 *Frank: A Sequel to Frank in Early Lessons.*

1823 June, visits Scott in Edinburgh. August, spends fortnight as Scott's guest at Abbotsford.

1825 *Harry and Lucy Concluded: Being the Last Part of Early Lessons.* First collected edition of works. August, Scott visits Edgeworthstown.

1826 *Thoughts on Bores.*

1827 *Little Plays for Children,* three plays.

1829 *Gary-Owen: Or the Snow-woman,* in *Christmas Box.* September, Wordsworth visits Edgeworthstown.

1830 Visits England.

1832 *Poor Bob the Chimney-sweeper.* Second collected edition of works.

1833 Visits Conemara.

1834   *Helen,* last novel.

1840   Visits England.

1843   Final visit to England.

1848   *Orlandino,* a short temperance story for young people.

1849   Maria Edgeworth dies on 22 May.

Chapter One
The Family Legacy

Few readers of fiction today are familiar with the range and variety of Maria Edgeworth's writings. In addition to ten major novels for adults, her fiction also includes several volumes of stories for children, and short stories and novelettes for young people and adults. She is the author (or coauthor with her father) of educational works, a biography, studies of Irish language and culture, nonfictional essays, literary criticism, and drama for children and adults. This widely varied oeuvre reflects a large range of personal interests and experiences and the cumulative effect of the Edgeworth family history. Most particularly, it reflects an unusual collaboration with her father, Richard Lovell Edgeworth, which lasted until his death in 1817. He hoped that he and his daughter were "considered as acting, and working, and thinking in concert."[1] And in the middle of her most productive years, she considered him the moving force behind her creative efforts: "Seriously it was to please my Father I first exerted myself to write, to please him I continued."[2] The ideas that inform her fiction and the purposes that infuse it most often reflect his life experience. It is impossible to understand her achievement as a novelist without first knowing something of her father.

Richard Lovell Edgeworth

The best account of Richard Lovell Edgeworth's life is found in his own *Memoirs,* begun by himself in 1808 and concluded by Maria[3] after his death. Aside from detailing his own remarkable achievements, the *Memoirs* suggest that at least four phases of his experience influenced his daughter: the family side of his life, including his ancestry and education and his role as husband and father; his mechanical and scientific interests, which led to a family association with some of the most famous scientists and educators of his day; his pioneering educational achievements, reflected in two major educational works written jointly with his daughter; and his sociopolitical experience, seen in his role as Irish landlord, educator, and politician and reflected in three of Maria's novels, *The Absentee, Ennui,* and *Ormond.*

Richard Lovell Edgeworth's family first came to Ireland from England during the reign of Queen Elizabeth. His ancestors, typical of the newly established Anglo-Irish gentry, were transplants in an alien country, having little in common with its customs and traditions. Typical, too, was a family history of extravagance, dissipation and gambling, marriages for convenience, absenteeism, and mismanagement of land and money. Edgeworth described his grandfather, "Protestant Frank," as a "loyal man and zealous Protestant" who "married successively several wives," and who "was involved in difficulties by his own taste for play."[4] His affairs were in such disarray at his death that his son would have lost the whole property without the assistance of a wise guardian.

Edgeworth's father gradually restored the family fortunes, partly by his success as a lawyer, partly by his marriage in 1732 to Jane Lovell, daughter of a Welsh judge. Edgeworth described his father as "upright, honourable, sincere, and sweet-tempered" and remembered the example of "perfect morality, and of unaffected piety" which he set for his children. His mother treated him as a reasonable being and warned him early about excesses of passion and temper. She taught him to read from the Old Testament and Aesop's fables and inspired him with a "love for truth, a dislike of low company, and an admiration for whatever was generous." After a few months preparatory training in Latin grammar at home, the eight-year-old boy was sent to school, and his next eight years were divided between formal lessons and interests developed during school holidays. His passion for sports was soon extinguished by a taste for reading, which he retained until the end of his life.

At sixteen, Edgeworth entered Trinity College, Dublin, where for six months he neglected his studies and passed his time in dissipation. Heavy drinking was the fashion of the day, and by the end of his stay he had become disgusted by the deplorable manner in which he had conducted himself. He had earlier freed himself from the vice of gambling and now considered himself cured of the weakness of intoxication. His father now decided to remove him to Oxford, principally because Paul Elers, an old family friend, could act as family guardian. During three years at Oxford, young Edgeworth was able to combine serious discipline in his studies with an entertaining social life. Vacations at Bath first exposed him to the world of fashion—the world of Beau Nash and Lord Chesterfield—and to the society of agreeable young ladies with whom he danced and conversed. All his observations on female manners and morals and character mattered little at this time, however, for he had become "insensibly entangled" with Paul Elers's eldest daughter, Anna Maria. Finding no honorable means of extrication, he eloped with her to Scotland, where they were married in 1763. A few months afterward, his disppointed father consented to the marriage and had him remarried by license.

Although Richard Lovell Edgeworth was married four times and the father of twenty-two children, his first marriage to Anna Maria Elers, the mother of Maria, was his only unhappy one. According to Edgeworth, his wife was ill-tempered and lamented about trifles. The birth of his first child (a son) in 1764, before he was twenty, ended his Oxford career, and soon afterward the ill-matched couple set off for Edgeworthstown. His mother died soon after their arrival, but her parting advice made a lasting impression: "My son, learn how to say No" (the later motto for *Vivian*). She further cautioned him "to finish never procrastinate." He found in her example a model of female virtue which his daughter would later use as a basis for her heroines: a rational mind cultivated by wide reading in literature, history, and religion; a firm yet generous and forgiving disposition; and a character that combined good sense and sound judgment in educating her children.

The family returned to England in the autumn of 1765 and settled in Hare Hatch, a small village about thirty-five miles west of London. Here Edgeworth set up a workshop for mechanical experiments, an early indication of his interest in science and technology which his daughter Maria would eventually share. When he went to London to keep term at the Temple, he was introduced through his wife's relations to a number of polite and well-informed people and to men of letters and science. It was at this time that he met Sir Francis Delaval, a fashionable rake and fortune hunter. A two-year acquaintance with Delaval convinced Edgeworth that "a life of pleasure is not a life of happiness," that public gaiety often means private ennui. These negative views determined his notions of fashion until his death, and his daughter's, too, for most of her life. Two days before his death, Delaval confided his regrets about the futility of a life of folly, and many years later Maria would rely on a number of his character traits for Lady Delacour in *Belinda*.

Edgeworth now turned his attention to the construction of carriages and after successfully completing a phaeton, designed on a principle used by Erasmus Darwin, wrote Darwin to inform him of its approval by the Society for the Encouragement of Arts. Darwin, assuming that Edgeworth was a coachmaker, invited him for a visit to Lichfield. In the summer of 1766, Edgeworth accepted the invitation, and the prolonged visit marked an important turning point in his career. Erasmus Darwin was an able physician, judged by the professional standards of his day, and a brilliant amateur mechanic and poet. Through Darwin, Edgeworth met Matthew Boulton, James Keir, William Small, James Watt, and Josiah Wedgewood, names now less familiar to the student of literature than to the historian of science. Together they formed part of the nucleus of the Lunar Society of Birmingham, which more than any other group represented the progressive forces of change in late eighteenth-century England. They were men of broad social and cultural interests, but their major mutual interest was science and the application of science to industry. Edgeworth found in the group both intellectual stimulus and support for his pioneering inventions; equally important, he formed lifelong friendships with Darwin, Wedgewood, Keir, and Watt with whom he continued to correspond long after he settled in the intellectually remote village of Edgeworthstown.

His interest in education was encouraged by another lifelong friend, Thomas Day, whom he met in 1766. Day has come down to us largely as a colorful eccentric, heavy and unkempt in appearance, somber, philosophical, and droll. But these traits were insignificant to a friendship that spanned twenty years. What Edgeworth saw in Day was an idealized portrait of the independent man, who wanted to serve and reform mankind, and who had sufficient courage to support unpopular opinion and to live an unconventional life in support of his convictions. Edgeworth and Day were both interested in Rousseau. Edgeworth had already decided to rear his eldest son, Richard, according to the principles of *Emile.* Between the ages of three and eight the child was left largely to nature and accident. He grew hardy and robust and generous; but the experiment fared badly, and even Rousseau admitted partial failure when the child was introduced to him seven years later.

Day also embarked on an ill-fated educational experiment, the training of a wife to meet his own qualifications. Edgeworth's experience with Rousseau's system considerably modified his thinking on

Chapter One
The Family Legacy

Few readers of fiction today are familiar with the range and variety of Maria Edgeworth's writings. In addition to ten major novels for adults, her fiction also includes several volumes of stories for children, and short stories and novelettes for young people and adults. She is the author (or coauthor with her father) of educational works, a biography, studies of Irish language and culture, nonfictional essays, literary criticism, and drama for children and adults. This widely varied oeuvre reflects a large range of personal interests and experiences and the cumulative effect of the Edgeworth family history. Most particularly, it reflects an unusual collaboration with her father, Richard Lovell Edgeworth, which lasted until his death in 1817. He hoped that he and his daughter were "considered as acting, and working, and thinking in concert."[1] And in the middle of her most productive years, she considered him the moving force behind her creative efforts: "Seriously it was to please my Father I first exerted myself to write, to please him I continued."[2] The ideas that inform her fiction and the purposes that infuse it most often reflect his life experience. It is impossible to understand her achievement as a novelist without first knowing something of her father.

Richard Lovell Edgeworth

The best account of Richard Lovell Edgeworth's life is found in his own *Memoirs,* begun by himself in 1808 and concluded by Maria[3] after his death. Aside from detailing his own remarkable achievements, the *Memoirs* suggest that at least four phases of his experience influenced his daughter: the family side of his life, including his ancestry and education and his role as husband and father; his mechanical and scientific interests, which led to a family association with some of the most famous scientists and educators of his day; his pioneering educational achievements, reflected in two major educational works written jointly with his daughter; and his sociopolitical experience, seen in his role as Irish landlord, educator, and politician and reflected in three of Maria's novels, *The Absentee, Ennui,* and *Ormond.* Richard Lovell Edgeworth's family first came to Ireland from England during the reign of Queen Elizabeth. His ancestors, typical of the newly established Anglo-Irish gentry, were transplants in an alien country, having little in common with its customs and traditions. Typical, too, was a family history of extravagance, dissipation and gambling, marriages for convenience, absenteeism, and mismanagement of land and money. Edgeworth described his grandfather, "Protestant Frank," as a "loyal man and zealous Protestant" who "married successively several wives," and who "was involved in difficulties by his own taste for play."[4] His affairs were in such disarray at his death that his son would have lost the whole property without the assistance of a wise guardian.

Edgeworth's father gradually restored the family fortunes, partly by his success as a lawyer, partly by his marriage in 1732 to Jane Lovell, daughter of a Welsh judge. Edgeworth described his father as "upright, honourable, sincere, and sweet-tempered" and remembered the example of "perfect morality, and of unaffected piety" which he set for his children. His mother treated him as a reasonable being and warned him early about excesses of passion and temper. She taught him to read from the Old Testament and Aesop's fables and inspired him with a "love for truth, a dislike of low company, and an admiration for whatever was generous." After a few months preparatory training in Latin grammar at home, the eight-year-old boy was sent to school, and his next eight years were divided between formal lessons and interests developed during school holidays. His passion for sports was soon extinguished by a taste for reading, which he retained until the end of his life.

At sixteen, Edgeworth entered Trinity College, Dublin, where for six months he neglected his studies and passed his time in dissipation. Heavy drinking was the fashion of the day, and by the end of his stay he had become disgusted by the deplorable manner in which he had conducted himself. He had earlier freed himself from the vice of gambling and now considered himself cured of the weakness of intoxication. His father now decided to remove him to Oxford, principally because Paul Elers, an old family friend, could act as family guardian. During three years at Oxford, young Edgeworth was able to combine serious discipline in his studies with an entertaining social life. Vacations at Bath first exposed him to the world of fash-

education when he later began to codify his principles on training and educating children. Day's experiment formed the basis for the wife-training episode in *Belinda*. A ten-year correspondence between Edgeworth and Day about the education of women was the foundation for the first portion of *Letters for Literary Ladies*. And Day's austere disapproval of female authorship and Edgeworth's deference for his friend's judgment prevented Maria from publishing until after Day's death in 1789.

The visit to Darwin in Lichfield was to have other consequences for Edgeworth. The literary coterie of the town centered around the home of Thomas Seward, canon of Lichfield. This congenial gathering included Darwin, Small, Kier, and Boulton and was open to Edgeworth whenever he chose to visit. The attraction was not the canon, but the canon's daughter Anna, the famous "Swan of Lichfield," and her pupil Honora Sneyd. Edgeworth and Day both made the mistake of falling in love with Honora. Edgeworth saw in her the image of female perfection that existed in his imagination, and fearing his growing fondness for her, resolved to go abroad. In the autumn of 1771 he left his wife and children with his mother-in-law and set out for France, accompanied by his son Richard, a child of eight, and Mr. Day. During his stay in France, which lasted almost two years, he learned French, studied practical mechanics, and engaged in a project for enlarging the city of Lyons by diverting the course of the Rhone. In 1772 his wife joined him for the summer and returned with Day to England that autumn. His wife died in March 1773, and within four months he married Honora Sneyd and left for Ireland.

For almost three years he and his family lived in domestic retirement in Edgeworthstown. In 1776 they returned to England and settled at North Church near Great Berkhamstead. It was here that the Edgeworths' family work in education was founded. Eventually, Maria would become a partner in the work and value it even more highly than her own fiction. Consequently, it is important to understand the system of teaching and educational theory which Edgeworth and Honora developed during the crucial years of 1776–79. The experiment with Richard having failed, Edgeworth turned away from Rousseau to find another educational approach. His thinking was now increasingly shaped by attitudes of the Lunar group. Bolton, Watt, Kier, and Small concerned themselves not only with advances in science and technology, but they shared forward-looking and progressive attitudes toward education as well. In general they criticized the uselessness of public education because of its remoteness from the business of life and its moral worthlessness. Edgeworth agreed with Joseph Priestley that the curriculum must be liberalized to include modern history, policy, arts, mathematics, commerce, and science. In *Practical Education* he and Maria would state strongly his criticisms of rote methods of learning, the narrow classical curriculum of the contemporary grammar and public school, and the failure of the system to account for individual differences.

From Priestley, Edgeworth also absorbed Hartley's theory of the association of ideas: the belief that since the mind is formed by circumstances, ideas become associated together in a certain order in the mind, and by organizing a child's experiences according to a definite pattern, it was possible to exercise a formative influence on his mental development. Basic to scientific experiment was the belief that Nature is governed by laws that could be discovered. There must also be laws governing the human mind. If these could be discovered, education could become an experimental science. Maria would later claim for her father the distinction of being the first to practice the experimental method in education. It was against this background that Edgeworth and Honora began to collect data for a study of children, based on actual experience. Their goal was to develop a system to teach their own children to read, one that would stress the child's capacity to reason and account for individual differences. Their conclusions would thus be based on actual teaching, as opposed to educational theory. In order to establish facts about what real children could learn and know, they conducted experimental lessons with the children. Honora kept a register of Edgeworth's questions and explanations, and the answers of the children. As a result, in 1779 they began a story about two children, Harry and Lucy. Its purpose was to plant the seeds of science and morality in the mind of a young child, and its method was to follow the natural process by which the mind developed. In general, its content and approach formed the basis for Maria's *Early Lessons* and inspired her classic stories for children in *The Parent's Assistant*.

Edgeworth and Honora's joint efforts were halted by her declining health. She had earlier shown a tendency toward consumption, but the signs were now unmistakable. A succession of moves and repeated visits to the best doctors available were of no avail. Honora died on 1 May 1780. On her deathbed she advised her husband to marry again and suggested her sister Elizabeth as an agreeable companion. In spite of scandal created by marriage to a deceased wife's sister; in spite of family opposition on both sides and bad publicity that reached as far as Birmingham; and in spite of ecclesiastical threats from the bishop of Lichfield, Edgeworth and Elizabeth were quietly married in St. Andrew's Church, London, on Christmas day, 1780.

Edgeworth's third marriage would have important consequences for the family since Elizabeth wisely established rapport with her new stepchildren and brought them closer to their father. Within a year of his marriage he made another decision even more momentous: to return to Ireland, possibly the "best possession of her British Majesty."

If Richard Lovell Edgeworth's career had ended at this point, he would still deserve considerably more recognition than he has received. His own singular account of his inventions—a wooden horse for climbing walls; a carriage that "should carry a road for itself"; a large umbrella for covering haystacks; a machine for cutting turnips; a machine for "measuring the force exerted by horses in drawing ploughs and waggons"—obscures the importance that his contemporaries placed on his inventions. The Society of Arts awarded him a silver medal in 1768 and a gold medal in 1769 for his contributions; and eleven years later he was selected for membership in the Royal Society. From 1766 to 1776, when mechanics and the Lunar Society exerted their greatest impact, he had contributed significantly to the design and construction of vehicles and made experiments with the portable telegraph that predated Chappé in France by some twenty-five years. From 1776 to 1779 he had laid the foundation for the family's future work in education. It was now time to change status from Irish absentee to resident landlord. In June 1782, Edgeworth and Elizabeth, accompanied by children of three marriages, set out for Ireland. It marked the beginning of a new life—and the making of a novelist named Maria Edgeworth.

Maria Edgeworth

Maria Edgeworth was born on 1 January 1768[5] at Black Bourton, Oxon, the third child and eldest daughter of Richard Lovell Edgeworth and his first wife, Anna Maria Elers. Because of her parents' marital discord, the first five important years of her life were loosely supervised. Years later, her father would stress the need for close parental supervision, but the thought does not seem to have occurred to him during Maria's formative years. She remembered little about the family's residence at Lichfield, but she recalled vividly her mother's death and "being taken into the room to receive her last kiss."[6] After her mother's death in 1773, she went with her father and stepmother Honora Sneyd to Ireland. Honora did not yet have children of her own, but she theorized that a child's character must be formed in infancy and that the right moment had already been lost with Maria. The stepmother did not take kindly to the ill-behaved child who cut out squares in a checked sofa cover and trampled through a number of hot-bed frames.

In the autumn of 1775, she was sent to Mrs. Latuffiere's school in Derby where she excelled in penmanship, French, Italian, and embroidery. But she did not make any significant friendships here, and her parents' letters, her only contacts with home, did little to relieve her anxiety and loneliness. In 1778 her father expressed hope that she would become "an amiable girl . . . with a benevolent heart, complying temper, and obliging manners" and suggested that her person would be "exactly in the middle point, between beauty and plainness—handsome enough to be upon a level with the generality of your sex, if accompanied with gentleness, reserve, and real good sense—plain enough to become contemptible, if unattended with good qualities of the head and heart."[7] The suggestion made a lasting impression on the woman to be. Well into her adult years she remained painfully conscious of her diminutive size and plainness. Fifty years later she wrote to her American friend, Mrs. Lazarus: "There is no picture of me. . . . My face has nothing remarkable in it of any kind nor has it any expression such as you would expect; therefore I would rather you took your idea of me from my writings."[8]

Early in 1781 Maria was sent to Mrs. Devis's school, a fashionable establishment in Upper Wimpole Street, London. If she had been unhappy at Mrs. Latuffiere's, she was now even more miserable, surrounded as she was by pretty, fashionable girls who were being educated for good marriages. But she was an excellent student, preparing her lessons a full quarter in advance and spending her remaining time reading for pleasure. She was also a good storyteller, and at both schools she entertained her classmates with amusing stories, sometimes making them up as she went along. Two years earlier, her father had sent the eleven-year-old Maria her first writing assignment, a two-page summary of an Arabian fable which she was to complete. In May 1780 he sent a second request for a short tale about generosity which must not be based on either history or romance. The same subject was given to an Oxford student, and when the two stories were completed and judged by Edgeworth's brother-in-law, Maria's was pronounced the best.

Edgeworth's requests for stories had stemmed from his daughter's rather dispirited and colorless letters home. He asked her to write familiarly, to share her likes and dislikes, so that their relationship could be more firmly established. The subject of letter writing preoccupied her throughout most of her life. Sensitive to her father's early criticism, she consciously strove to develop a confidential and pleasing style. She believed strongly that sharing or publishing letters led to affectation in writing and to the destruction of private confidence.

Her two holiday visits to the home of Thomas Day in 1781 must have further reinforced her serious image of herself and her distaste for female accomplishments, the obsession at Mrs. Devis's fashionable school. Day had at last married a Miss Milnes, who shared his peculiar thinking about an austere and severely secluded way of life. At Day's house Maria was allowed access to an excellent library and trained in speculative and philosophic lessons that demanded perfect accuracy in her answers. In the summer of this year, she had begun to suffer from an acute inflammation of the eyes, and one doctor had brutally told her that she would go blind. The threat of blindness at last brought her to the full attention of her father, and his letters during the late summer and autumn of 1781 express both affection and concern. Within a few short months, he had resolved to dedicate the remainder of his life to the improvement of his estate and the education of his children. When the family arrived in Edgeworthstown in June 1782, a painfully insecure and timid fourteen-year-old Maria was becoming part of a family which ever afterward remained the center of her existence.

Life in Ireland: 1782–1817

During the early 1780s Edgeworth's interests in science and mechanics necessarily took second place to the management of his estate, his duties as landlord and magistrate, and the education of his children. The loss of his wife Honora had left a painful void. His new wife, Elizabeth, was an excellent helpmate and companion, but by 1784 she was the mother of four children of her own in as many

years, and during the next ten years would bear five more—although
only three of the five survived infancy. At this time Edgeworth found
in Maria the intellectual challenge that he needed, and from 1782 to
1784 she received a more concentrated attention from him than at
any other period of her life. From these years stem her obsessive
dependency and her frequent tributes to the "father who educated
me; to whom, under Providence, I owe all of good or happiness I
have enjoyed in life."[9] What he taught her, as his assistant and book-
keeper, and what they together observed about rural Ireland, through
English eyes, is fundamental to an understanding of the Irish novels.

Dublin in 1782 was becoming a beautiful city full of handsome
town houses and imposing public buildings—a city of rakes and fashion and elegance. But in the remote countryside, things were different, and Edgeworth's work was already cut out for him. His father
had died in 1770, and he had been an absentee for seven of the in-
tervening twelve years. The care of the estate had been left to agents
who had considerably reduced its value through profiteering. The
family house was damp and dilapidated, and the want of painting,
glazing, roofing, and fencing was everywhere apparent. Flocks of tenants begged an audience for grievances, secret claims, accusations,
and tales of distress.[10] Edgeworth knew that a solution could be realized only through principles of wise management over a long period
of time.

In her father's *Memoirs,* Maria describes in detail what her father
tried to accomplish in 1782. In order to secure managerial control of
the estate, he eliminated the middleman and asked that rents be paid
directly to himself or to his family.[11] Without this intervention he
was able to establish a new relationship between landlord and tenant.
He became individually acquainted with his tenants and their varying
circumstances and through them learned the real value of his land.
He eventually gained their confidence and loyalty by eliminating past
abuses. He rewarded tenants who improved cottages and land and encouraged their exertion and initiative by limiting the length of leases.
He abolished the oppressive claims of duty-work and duty-fowl and
omitted a number of feudal fines and penalties from the leases. He
retained the alienation fine, which enabled him to keep quality tenants and to prevent middlemen from fleecing tenants with unreasonable rents. He exercised firmness whenever it was required and in
general adopted a course of moderation and good sense. If he erred,
it was probably on the side of generosity. As his old steward ex-

pressed it, "He's only afraid of himself being too good,—and he's right enough there."[12]

The year 1782 also marked the first of Edgeworth's two phases of political activity in Ireland. The Irish Volunteers had been formed in Belfast early in 1779 to defend Ireland against threatened invasion at a time when British troops were involved in the American Revolutionary War. Others quickly followed the Belfast lead, and corps were soon established in each county. The Patriots recognized the political advantage of their position, and between 1779 and 1783 they used their power for effective reform. They achieved a measure of Catholic emancipation and the removal of restrictions on trade; and they brought about the establishment of an independent Irish parliament in Dublin. Although Edgeworth attended the National Convention of Volunteers as a delegate from County Longford, his major contribution seems to have been the relatively minor role he played in peacefully terminating the Volunteer Assembly. Maria did not see it that way, for she was extremely proud of her father's political activities during 1782–83 and gives them full weight in his *Memoirs*. What she omits to say is that by 1784 the cause of reform had passed to a less respectable landless class. In sympathizing with the cause, Edgeworth detached himself from prevailing attitudes of the Anglo-Irish gentry, a detachment that his daughter would explore in full in her Irish fiction.

With the dissolution of the Convention, Edgeworth now turned his attention more fully to the care and education of his growing family. He read aloud to them from Shakespeare, Milton, and Homer and encouraged them to read on subjects they could understand—biography, travels, literature, and science. He continued the experimental lessons with his children and now gave Maria the task of keeping careful records of his questions and of the children's responses. In the autumn of 1782, he had set Maria the task of translating Madame de Genlis's *Adèle et Théodore,* but she had completed only one volume when Thomas Holcroft's translation appeared. Working on the translation, however, brought her into direct collaboration with her father for the first time and established him in the role of editor and literary adviser. In 1785 Edgeworth was elected a member of the newly formed Royal Irish Academy, which stressed the practical development of agriculture and industry, and during the next two years occupied himself with agricultural improvements and mechanical projects, including a successful wooden moveable railway for the conveyance of limestone gravel. Maria's time was occupied with the education of her young brother Henry, entrusted to her charge, and with an impressive program of reading in constitutional law, political economy, history, travel, and biography. The 1790s opened and closed with a visit to England. In the summer of 1791 Edgeworth and his wife left for Bristol and for the first time in nine years, Maria was separated from her father and from the security and protection which she treasured. Edgeworth's favorite sister, Margaret Ruxton, provided her with the parent figure she needed. Part of Mrs. Ruxton's attraction was her family resemblance to her brother, a resemblance that Maria pointed out on many occasions. Mrs. Ruxton not only served as Maria's friend and confidante, but became her chief literary adviser and critic during the early 1800s and the inspiration behind some of her fiction, including *Castle Rackrent*. Maria wrote to Aunt Ruxton freely and without reserve, and her letters—especially during the 1790s—reveal a sensitive, witty, chatty human being, a solicitous and loyal daughter and sister, and a sympathetic observer of human nature. They also show the uncertainties and doubts and anxieties, the least glamorous but more human side that earlier biographers have tended to obscure.

In October 1791, Maria joined her parents in Clifton for a two-year stay in England. During the following autumn, her visit to Mrs. Charles Hoare, a former schoolgirl friend now living near London, would be her only firsthand exposure to fashionable society before her major tales of fashionable life were completed. The visit only confirmed her worst suspicions about the evils of high society and her distaste for its insincerity and artificiality. Her attitudes toward London society were somewhat modified after her father's death, but her changed views came too late to affect the decidedly negative views of her fiction.

Back at Edgeworthstown in 1793, she finished her first two works for publication. Thomas Day had died in 1789 and Edgeworth's ban on publication, made in deference to Day's views, had long since been lifted. It seemed appropriate that the influence of her father's close friend should inspire her first published work, *Letters for Literary Ladies* (1795). It was followed the next year by the first volume of *The Parent's Assistant*, stories for children which established her lasting reputation in this genre. The large amount of writing that she did for *Practical Education*, the Edgeworths' *magnum opus* on education, brought an even closer collaboration with her father. By 1797

she had completed her masterpiece, *Castle Rackrent,* which neither she nor her father afterward preferred. Ironically, she had little notion of its literary value nor of the value of her more imaginative children's stories. She thought the greatest accomplishment of the 1790s was her father's experimental work on education and the stories which had been directly inspired by its theories.

The family's return to Ireland in 1793 was prompted by newspaper accounts of internal disturbances. Rumors of French invasion and the need for an effective means of communication within the country encouraged Edgeworth to devote his full energies to the telegraph. In a public experiment in August 1794, he successfully transmitted telegraphic messages across the channel from Ireland to Scotland. There is little doubt that he failed to receive proper recognition for his work at this time. When the alarm of invasion subsided, government authorities lost interest in the invention, and he turned his attention to other matters. In February 1796 he canvassed unsuccessfully for one of the two County Longford seats. And in 1797 his activities were suspended by the declining health and death of his wife Elizabeth, who, like her sister before her, died of consumption.

His household now consisted of nine children: four sons and five daughters, and two maiden sisters of his late wife. As early as 1774, Edgeworth had met Daniel Augustus Beaufort, the clergyman and distinguished cartographer and topographer. His daughter Frances had sketched some designs for *The Parent's Assistant.* When she visited Edgeworthstown with her parents in 1798, Edgeworth was persuaded that she would ensure his own happiness and the happiness of his family; and on 31 May 1798—his fifty-fourth birthday—he married the twenty-nine-year-old Frances Ann Beaufort. Even Maria was shocked at the thought of her father's marrying a woman a year younger than herself, but she soon agreed that he had made a good choice.

When Edgeworth and his new bride set out from Dublin to Edgeworthstown, rebellion had broken out in many parts of the country. Near Enfield, they passed a carriage turned up; a man hung between the shafts, murdered by insurgents. By autumn 1798, nationwide insurrection seemed imminent. People were leagued in secret rebellion, waiting only for the arrival of the French army before engaging in open violence. Corrupt magistrates scoured the countryside, ignoring the law and imprisoning the innocent. Although the principal gentry of County Longford had raised corps of yeomanry, Edgeworth had delayed doing so, believing that civil authority was preferable to military interference and force. But now, to protect his own tenantry, he had no choice. He recruited both Protestants and Catholics, arousing suspicions from those who warned him of Catholic betrayal. The French fleet arrived in County Mayo in August 1798, and after defeating a large Anglo-Irish army at Castlebar, advanced eastward toward County Longford. Edgeworth's infantry was without arms and desperate. The family was sent ahead, and Edgeworth commanded his defenseless corps to march to Longford. Suspected by the loyalist Orange yeomanry of Longford, he was asked to expel the corps, but he dared not abandon them to the rebel-infested countryside. When the French danger had passed, following the Anglo-Irish victory near Granard, a sergeant raised a mob at Longford and denounced Edgeworth and his family as traitors. The family was soon able to return home safely, but the advantages of living in civilized England now seemed more persuasive than ever. Although Edgeworth brought charges against the sergeant of the Longford Corps of Infantry, he did not press trial. His father-in-law convinced him that to leave Ireland would be to acquiesce to false charges and thereby lose what he had fought to preserve.

Since Maria would draw heavily on her father's political experience for the Irish novels, it is necessary to examine briefly the sources of his social and political conflicts in County Longford. As preceding biographical details have shown, he had spent over fifteen years among some of the best-educated and most progressive English thinkers of the time. In a remote rural Irish village he was a model landlord, both in the treatment of his tenants and in the management of his estate. He could believe at the same time in Catholic emancipation and ascendancy rule. He hated war but sought to protect his country against the French. He denounced political corruption and sectarian bias, recruited both Catholics and Protestants for his infantry, and worked for the improvement of the poor and underprivileged. It is not surprising that his neighbors, who interpreted problems in political and religious terms, viewed him with suspicion. Upon reflection, he realized that he had been misunderstood in part because of the relative social isolation in which he and his family had lived. After his fourth marriage he circulated more freely with his neighbors, and his family found a normal social life with other members of the gentry.

A few months before his fourth marriage, Edgeworth was elected to the Irish Parliament for the borough of St. John's Town and began his second major phase of political activity. According to Maria, his two principal objectives were to forward educational reform and participate in discussion of the Union. In a speech to the assembled Parliament in 1799, he pleaded for parliamentary intervention in removing the oppressive defects of public education. He urged the establishment of one or more schools in each parish, the examination and licensing of masters, and the inspection of schools at least once a year. As a result of these efforts, the Duke of Bedford set up a board of commissioners to investigate the best means of educating children of the lower classes. During his four years of service on the board, Edgeworth offered many clear-sighted views on means of reforming prevailing abuses. He carefully pointed out the need to safeguard the religious beliefs of both Catholics and Protestants, at the same time giving Catholics the quality of education that would prepare them for professional advancement.

In the spring of 1799, Edgeworth, his wife Elizabeth, and Maria visited England again for a few months, but the visit made little contribution to Maria's experience as a writer. Not only were her literary contacts limited, but her journey through the industrial Midlands—so significant to the novelists of the 1840s—made little impression. Her forte would be people, not places. Edgeworth returned to Ireland in the autumn of 1799 to find the country in bitter controversy over legislative union between Britain and Ireland. In principle, he believed that Union would benefit Ireland's commercial interests and that Pitt would favor equal votes for Catholics after the measure passed. But he voted against it because it was being forced on a majority who opposed it and because of illegal means used to bring it about. Edgeworth himself was offered three thousand guineas for his seat during the last remaining weeks of the session and tempted by attractive inducements for his family and friends. His vote against the Union was his last great public and political gesture.

Edgeworth lived for seventeen years after the Union. These comparatively quiet years were devoted to traveling abroad and entertaining at home, to supervising his daughter's works for publication, and to his agricultural and mechanical interests. In the autumn of 1802, following the Peace of Amiens, he decided to visit Paris. The Edgeworths were not unknown in France. In 1798–99, Charles Pictet-de-Rochemont had published a French version of *Practical Education* in the *Bibliothèque Britannique,* a literary and scientific periodical that served as an important cultural link between England and the Continent. His brother, Marc-Auguste Pictet, had visited the family in the summer of 1802 and invited them for a visit. Through Pictet, Edgeworth would have an introduction to the best society of Paris. And he made it no secret that he hoped his daughter would find a husband. As it turned out, Maria received her only proposal of marriage in Paris. Abraham Niclas Clewberg Edelcrantz, private secretary to the king of Sweden, and well known in his own country as an inventor and patron of the arts, offered her his hand and heart. She had known him for less than a month, much too short a time to persuade her to leave her father and family to live in Sweden. Yet there seems little doubt that she was very much in love with him and long afterward could be moved to tears by the unexpected mention of his name, or even of Sweden, in a book or newspaper. She had once implied to her brother Sneyd that she would like to have a husband and children. She was now thirty-four and probably realized that this would be her only proposal. Back home in 1804 she began writing *Leonora* with the hope of pleasing Edelcrantz. Her stepmother records that it was "written in a style which he liked, and the idea of what he would think of it was . . . present to her in every page she wrote."[13] She never saw Edelcrantz again. He died, unmarried, in 1821.

In the spring of 1813 the family visited England for the last time before Edgeworth's death. The second series of *Tales of Fashionable Life* had appeared the previous year, and Maria's reputation as a writer was assured. The stay in London lasted for only six weeks, but the long list of people she met from the world of rank and fashion reads like a social register. She met Byron's future mother-in-law and wife and recorded that "Lady Milbanke is very agreeable and has a charming well informed daughter."[14] Unfortunately, no account of her breakfast with the famous son-in-law and errant husband has been preserved. She obviously did not see in Byron the image he preserved for posterity and dryly observed that "his appearance is nothing that you would remark in any other man."[15] He said much more about her. She, was, he confessed, one of the "exhibitions" of 1813 in London, "a nice little unassuming 'Jeannie Deans-looking bodie,' " quiet in conversation, "and, if not handsome, certainly not ill-looking." Her father, on the other hand, was egotistical and talkative and "not much admired in London."[16] Other evidence from private correspondence of the time supports Byron's judgment that Edgeworth was unpopular in London. Literary men, at least, could not sympathize with the scientific and practical Edgeworth and thought him unimportant except as Maria's father. Following their return to Edgeworthstown, Maria at last completed *Patronage,* which had occupied her for four years, and collaborated with her father on additional work in education. By 1814, his health began to decline, and afterward her letters are filled with lengthy bulletins of his health. On 7 August 1815 an American Jewish woman, Rachel Mordecai Lazarus, wrote hesitantly to the famous Miss Edgeworth to complain of her unfavorable depiction of Jews. In response, Maria began to write *Harrington,* a sympathetic portrayal of Jews, the following year. But the writing proceeded slowly, and her father encouraged her to consider plans for other tales to be published at the same time. *Harrington,* finally finished in November 1816, filled only one volume, and her father's proposed solution was to publish the tale together with *Comic Dramas,* her first plays written for adults. She did not agree, for the plays were experiments which might suffer in comparison with the fiction. By February 1817 she was well along on a new novel which would supply the needed volume. Edgeworth was dying, and Maria realized how much the new work meant to her father. To some extent it represented the final test of her affection for him. It was also a test of character, "to finish, never procrastinate." By 16 February Mrs. Edgeworth was reading *Ormond* aloud to him, chapter by chapter, and Maria felt more than amply repaid for her labor and confinement. The novel, one of her most brilliant, had been written in three months. The family obtained an advance copy of the book for Edgeworth's birthday, but he did not live to see it published. During his final hours, he called each of the family members in for the farewell parting. What Maria perhaps remembered longest were his remarks to Mrs. Edgeworth: "I did not know how much I loved Maria till I came to the parting with her."[17]

The Literary Partnership

The greatest source of critical controversy about Maria Edgeworth is the role which her father played in her works. For the most part, critics and biographers have uniformly agreed that his influence was negative and blamed the artistic blemishes of the fiction on him. The literary partnership cannot be fairly judged outside the complex father-daughter personal relationship, the seeds of which were planted in Maria's childhood. Her emotional need for close family ties may be traced directly to the loneliness and neglect of her early years. They were years that she never forgot, and during the height of her fame she could write in gratitude to Aunt Ruxton as one "who has been constantly partially kind to me from the time I was a child with inflamed eyes and swelled features for whom nobody else cared."[18] Her physical plainness, coupled with a lively and capricious temperament, invited disciplinary measures that were both harsh and restrictive. As a child she did not develop either at school or at home any clearly recognized concept of her own personal identity. When her father began to supervise her education closely in 1782, she viewed her own importance either in relationship to him or to the family.

As we have seen, Richard Lovell Edgeworth had already established his principal beliefs about education by 1782. How he viewed his role as father, husband, and family member can be pieced together from his private letters. Central to his thinking was his belief that behavior is partially modified by rewards and punishments, a belief he practiced with consistency in his family. He complimented his third wife, Elizabeth, on female gentleness and efforts to please and took partial credit for his "skill and prognostic" in developing the person of his fourth wife, Frances. She felt that she had improved under his tutelage and wrote of her gratitude to Maria: "He has by valuing me taught me to value myself."[19] His influence over his favorite sister Margaret and her daughter Sophy was likewise pronounced. Whether in dealing with children or adults, Edgeworth viewed his family role primarily as educator, and one measure he used to ensure both loyalty and affection from his family was his stamp of personal approval through praise. How much his approbation meant to Maria is tedious to read about today. One of her letters, at least, exposes the real truth: "Do not give my love to my father—for he has more of it already than he knows what to do with—but that is his fault not mine—if he did not make me love him I should not love him—I believe—."[20] This is what Newby meant by his perceptive observation that Edgeworth "so conducted himself as to cause his daughter to love him uncritically and therefore adopt his precepts on literature and life unquestionably."[21] But it was clearly a two-way street.

Edgeworth characterized Maria's major character defect as "an inordinate desire to be beloved," the defect of the heroine of her final novel, published seventeen years after his death. His attitudes toward her at times reinforce her own image of herself and of the relationship with her father which she sought to preserve. But perhaps the most interesting aspect of the father-daughter relationship is the attitude of each toward the writings. Did Edgeworth, as his staunchest critics have maintained, use Maria as a mouthpiece for his own ideas? Did he consider her works as a means of enhancing his reputation? If we separate the writings on education from the fiction, the answer to the first question must surely be affirmative. *Practical Education* and *Professional Education,* the major works on education, prescribe a methodology for children and young adults which Edgeworth had developed in training his own large family. The publications were family projects, but most of the writing was done by Maria. The ideas were his. Likewise, in *Early Lessons, Moral Tales,* and *Popular Tales,* written to illustrate the principles of *Practical Education,* the ideas are primarily Edgeworth's.

The fiction for adults is another matter. In her father's *Memoirs* Maria says that she was free to use or reject his suggestions and that there was no danger of offending him by not using what he offered. The most common critical charges are that he censored the liveliest strain in his daughter, that he marred the novels by inserting passages, and that he made the fiction more didactic. If the autobiographical volume of Edgeworth's *Memoirs* is any indicator of personality, it is highly unlikely that a man so energetic and ebullient, so gifted with humor and wit, would have suppressed this tendency in another. The somber author of the novel's prefaces is not the man who emerges from the private letters. *Ormond* is the best authenticated source for Edgeworth's passages, since Maria made no secret of them. They are among the novel's liveliest.[22] The didacticism, characteristic of most of the fiction, seems to be peculiarly Maria's own. She could have found it in the moral tale of the time, but in general she was more influenced by what Edgeworth had taught her about character and conduct, and the example of family and friends, than by the intellectual stimulus of what she read.

What about the other charge—that Edgeworth enhanced his own reputation through his daughter? The answer depends on how we view his attitude toward fame. He was convinced that wealth and power did not lead to happiness, an attitude that recurs frequently in the fiction. His friend Erasmus Darwin encouraged him to publish; a book about new machines and inventions, Darwin suggested, would provide an avenue to fame. He did not follow Darwin's advice, and

Maria observed that his attitude toward fame was careless to a point
that would hardly be believed. Yet there are a few hints to the contrary. In 1812, he wrote from Dublin to his son Sneyd: "*Our* popu-
larity here is really more than we could have expected—You know
that it is *along with* Maria—but we share the triumph and partake the
gale of many a fawning admirer."[23] He suggested that the family trip
to England in 1813 be timed to coincide with the second series of
Tales of Fashionable Life. He considered some of his letters to Sneyd a
means of preserving the sentiments of old age, and some of them
seem designed more for a public than a private audience. Still, as
Marilyn Butler points out, his interest in his daughter's fiction was
clearly not proprietary.[24] He supervised details of publication, proof-
read her manusripts (as did other members of the family), supplied
her with abundant source material, and wrote prefaces to her fiction
because she asked him to. In the two works on education, he had said
essentially all that he had to say.

If the negative view of Richard Lovell Edgeworth has stemmed
partly from a misreading of his character, Maria's well-intentioned
but misleading interpretation of the partnership did not help. Her
major reason for writing was to please her father, but the pleasure
obviously meant something different to each. In her judgment, her
father interpreted her efforts as a "proof" of affection and gratitude,
but what she probably failed to understand is that he had found an
ideal means of motivating her to write. Her proof of affection was
demonstrated in completing a work in progress. Her reward was his
praise. He had taught her perfectly the lesson he learned from his
mother—"to finish, never procrastinate." On the other hand, her
pleasure was not entirely unselfish. Butler's perceptive conclusions
that she used the works—first, to continue intimacy with her father
during his lifetime—and later, to cement her relationship with her
family—seem absolutely justified by the family letters.[25] It was Maria
who hoped that placing the fiction within the frame of her father's
works on education would enhance his reputation. Except for the
works on education, the partnership was more real to her than to
him.

Edgeworth's most pronounced influence on his daughter's fiction is
the quality or texture of the thinking that went into it. Maria absorbed from her father the belief that education improves minds,
changes character, and prepares men and women to fulfill happy and
responsible roles in society. Edgeworth read widely in both classical

and modern literature, but he considered himself neither an author nor a man of letters. He was an educator, a scientist, and inventor who would have agreed with Darwin that a fool "is a man who never tried an experiment in his life." Basic to scientific experiment was the search for truth based on fact. And fact was central to teaching, the purpose of the joint works on education and the stories that supported them. Aside from these stories, Maria's preference for factual documentation was largely her own. Likewise, the rational, prudent heroine was a composite of her views about females in society. Admittedly, Edgeworth taught her that reason is a safe guide to conduct and cautioned her about temper, attention, and perseverance. But his lessons were intended as guides for her personal improvement, not as models of behavior for her heroines. He thought the tame, prudent Leonora one of her worst fictional creations and the "elegant, the lively, the useful, the correct and easy Griselda" one of her best. He asked her to read her own "Simple Susan," a children's classic, for improvement, and criticized the wife-rearing scheme in *Belinda*. In such judgments as these, his critical intelligence was clearly more perceptive than her own.

If he erred, it was probably the sin of omission. Maria fully absorbed his social, scientific, educational, and political beliefs. And although she learned much on her own from reading and firsthand observation, the changes in her attitudes occurred primarily after his death when the prime of her literary career was finished. On the level of plot, many of the tales and novels contain direct transcripts of his life experience. The English fiction is permeated with his ideas about marriage and female behavior, the disadvantages of fashionable society, the dangers of drink and gambling, and the evils of wealth and fortune. His ancestors and in-laws, his close friends and acquaintances often find parallels in Maria's characters. And the model parent or husband is often only Edgeworth in disguise.

From his approach as a scientist she developed an analytical, detached, impersonal habit of thinking, characteristic of most of her fiction. But what was a liability to her fashionable tales became an asset to her Irish fiction. The major themes of her Irish novels are the responsibilities of the Irish landlord; effective methods of improving Irish culture and educating the children of Irish peasants; and the problem of religious toleration. Her detailed, literal reporting of her father's Irish experience would make her seem much more significant as a novelist and much more relevant to her generation than any of her contemporaries. The freedom with which Edgeworth shared this experience with his daughter was finally his greatest gift of all.

The Later Years (1817–49)

Although Maria survived her father by three decades, her later years were comparatively unproductive. In the dozen or so years following her father's death, she did continue to write. She completed and published Edgeworth's *Memoirs* in 1820, and by 1825 had finished the sequels to *Early Lessons*. She considered and then discarded a number of sketches, and in 1830 finally set to work on *Helen,* her last novel for adults, published in 1834. After that she wrote only *Orlandino* (1848), a short temperance story for adolescents, as a contribution to the Irish Relief Fund. Her stepmother provided a family interpretation for her long silence: "She had long hesitated as to writing any work of fiction without that support and sanction to which she had been accustomed from her father in all her previous works . . . to write a tale which was to bear comparison with 'Belinda' or 'Patronage,' seemed to her for many years to be, without her father's encouragement, an impossibility."[26] This was the interpretation that she herself preferred.

But there were other reasons. During Edgeworth's lifetime, the family had lived in comfortable financial circumstances. At his death, the second eldest son Lovell had been entrusted with the management of the estate. By the end of 1825, he had encumbered the estate by debts that exceeded £25,000. From 1826 to 1839 Maria managed the estate with consummate skill and through courage and perseverance enabled her family to keep the land. In former years, her writings had been thoroughly revised and edited. But she now had less leisure for writing and less time for the careful revisions and corrections that she had always insisted on before publication.[27] She refers to both in a letter to her American friend Mrs. Lazarus: "I have very little time for writing for the public. . . . My publisher has written to ask me to give him another book, and I believe I shall. But I shall not hurry myself. . . . I have always thought it disgracefully mean in literary manufacturers to trade upon their name and to put off ill-finished works upon credit. That is what I never will do."[28] She had hoped to write another Irish novel, but the Ireland of *The Absentee, Ennui,* and *Ormond* had passed. O'Connell's repeal movement was alien to her inherited prejudices and loyalties. A Union of classes and creeds was no longer posible. She clung tenaciously to her father's political ideals—government by an enlightened elite, mutual cooperation between landlord and tenant, public and private devotion to duty. Writing about Ireland in the 1830s would have meant a change in her notions about social responsibility, a change she was never able to make.

Maria Edgeworth in middle and old age was neither the impersonal author of the novels nor the dependent daughter of the father whom she adored. Her letters home from England, Scotland, and the Continent are permeated by a warm, generous spirit, but they suggest that absences from her family are no longer a cause for anxiety and fear. The later decades were years of self-discovery and maturity, of self-confidence of a kind that she had never had during her father's lifetime. Yet this change in her personality, together with her increased contacts with an outside world of distinguished men and women, and her ambitious reading, did little to encourage her literary efforts. In 1837 she was working on a story but could not find a way to make it entertaining: "I am going on with Taking for Granted—I am ashamed to say how slowly. But I would rather write to my family and friends than for the public."[29] By 1847 she expressed most fully what she had been thinking all along. The publishers Simpkin and Marshall asked her to write prefaces for each story for a forthcoming edition of her works. In her letter to them, she concluded that whatever she might say no longer had relevance: "In truth I have nothing to say of them but what my dear father has said for me in his prefaces to each of them as they came out. These sufficiently explain the moral design; they require no national explanations, and I have nothing personal to add. As a woman, my life, wholly domestic, cannot afford anything interesting to the public: I am like the 'needy knifegrinder'—I have no story to tell."[30]

The remarks suggest that for all her brilliance as a story teller, she had never quite taken herself seriously as an author. They suggest, too, the inelasticity of her attitudes toward fiction at a time when the best writers and the reading public were seeing the larger possibilities of the novel as art. She preferred scientists over poets. And although her frequent observations on her contemporaries suggest an increasing critical awareness, it came too late to matter very much to her own fiction. She died on 22 May 1849.

Chapter Two
Education for Life

In her own time and throughout the nineteenth century, Maria Edgeworth was well-known as a writer for children, and historians of children's literature in this century have sometimes granted her the distinction of being the first realist writer for children in England.[1] Behind this reputation lies her pioneering work as an educational theorist. In concert with her father, she wrote two major treatises on pedagogy: *Practical Education* (1798), a step-by-step procedure for training and rearing children, and *Professional Education* (1809), a guidebook to training young men for professions. It is not surprising, given Richard Lovell Edgeworth's strong views on education and his experience in training a large family, that his daughter's fiction for children and adolescents should be written to illustrate his theories in *Practical Education*. And in principle, at least, she hoped that the fiction for adults would popularize his ideas on professional education. For Maria, the value of fiction was thus directly related to its power to instruct. For this reason, her father's prefaces describe the educational theses which her stories, tales, and novels propose to develop. A strong impulse behind the majority of her fiction thus derives from her desire to use it as an exploration of conduct. Her writings—addressed, as they are, to specific age groups and classes—undertake the education of mankind from infancy through adulthood.

Practical Education (1798)

In the autumn of 1798, *Practical Education* was published in two cumbersome quartos, and according to Maria's stepmother, the work was praised and criticized enough to make the authors immediately famous.[2] Certainly there was much to praise in a work that marked a milestone in the history of pedagogy. Twentieth-century scholars view it as the "most significant contemporary work on pedagogy,"[3] and one historian of education, in particular, claims that it is the most important work on general pedagogy to appear in Great Britain between the publication of Locke's *Thoughts* in 1693 and Herbert Spencer's *Essay on Education* in 1861.[4] At the time that *Practical Education* appeared, Britain needed practical reformers, and Richard Lovell Edgeworth was well qualified to help supply that need. His progressive theories on education, as we have seen, were largely shaped during his association with the Lunar Society. His own large family had provided an ideal laboratory for educational experiments. And all along, he had remained in touch with leading reform movements on the continent. In *Practical Education,* then, he and Maria were able to combine personal observations of child nature and behavior, deduced from experiment and application, with prevailing educational theories that had passed their own tests of practice and experiment.

As an educational treatise, *Practical Education* is a key to progressive eighteenth-century educational thought, combining as it does the best theories of Locke and Rousseau with a spirit of scientific inquiry. Locke's associationism provided a rational, materialist theory of learning that led to several conclusions: that man's mind is formed by circumstances; that education can change man's nature; that man is a rational being and capable of advancing to perfection; and that the child's mind can be formed through a patterned experience of education. Rousseau's influence on Edgeworth was perhaps even greater, for it was Rousseau's respect for the child's right to live a full life as a child, his realization of the difference between child and man, that revolutionized educational thought. Edgeworth rejected the principle of natural virtue because it had failed in practice with his eldest son, Richard. But he retained in original or modified form many of Rousseau's theories: the importance of parents, especially the mother, in ordering a child's environment; the stress on self-reliance and on "hardening" through experience; the preference for early private over public education; and especially the belief that education, to be effective in the making of good human beings and through them of a good society, must be child-centered. It was also Rousseau's stress on infancy, boyhood, and adolescence as stages in physical and mental development, each requiring special attention to change, that encouraged the Edgeworths to write fiction addressed to different age groups.

Practical Education is a basic handbook about learning and teaching, crowded with simple illustrations from family experience. The twenty-five essays in the book (including a summary) cover a wide range of learning experience: the mental faculties ("On Attention," "Memory and Invention," "Taste and Imagination," and "Wit and Judgment"); the curriculum ("Toys," "Tasks," "Books," "On Grammar and Classical Literature," "On Geography and Chronology," "On Arithmetic," "Geometry," "On Mechanics," and "Chemistry"); the controlled environment ("On Public and Private Education," "Servants," and "Acquaintance"); discipline ("On Obedience" and "On Rewards and Punishments"); and moral habits ("On Female Accomplishments, &c," "On Temper," "On Truth," "On Sympathy and Sensibility," "On Vanity, Pride, and Ambition," and "Prudence and Economy"). Although Maria did over half of the writing, most of the specialized chapters on curriculum were written by her father.

The general approach throughout is that learning should be a positive experience and that the discipline of education is more important during the formative years than the acquisition of knowledge. The temperate and enlightened attitudes toward punishment confirm the authors' outlook on childhood as a stage of natural and spontaneous happiness. The primary object of obedience is to make the child understand the connection that he believes and feels to exist between his social duties and social happiness. In developing the child's moral habits, the authors subscribe to Locke's conviction that knowledge is a fitting together of what is congruous and a separation of what is incongruous in the ideas supplied by experience. They agree with Rousseau that excessive severity and indulgence are to be equally avoided. And they concur with both Locke and Rousseau that lecturing children on maxims of morality is meaningless. In general, composure and equanimity are the objects in view, and achieving them depends on the parent or guardian's measured indulgence.

The chapters that describe the training of the child's mental faculties are likely to be of most interest to the modern reader for it is here that the authors probe most fully the psychology of childhood and learning. What can a child be expected to learn and know? What are his physical, mental, and moral limitations? In Richard Lovell Edgeworth's view, cultivating attention, memory, taste, and judgment, in that order, is the sum of the educative process. In general, the attention of the young child is developed through associations of time, place, and manner and through varied stimuli. As he grows older, "associated" attention is superseded by "voluntary" as he takes responsibility for his own success and improvement. Child memory should likewise be educated by well-trained associations, first of time and then of cause and effect. Rote learning is naturally condemned, for it blocks both the judgment and inventive faculty of the mind. The surest means of encouraging a child to feel that it is to his advantage to remember is to exercise his memory on things that are useful and agreeable to him in the business and amusement of daily life.

"Taste" and "Imagination" are used interchangeably to designate a formation of ideas, not images, grounded firmly on knowledge and experience. As we might expect, the authors are not concerned with taste (or elsewhere in the work, with "sympathy and sensibility") as a theory of aesthetics. Rather, the two principal components of taste, the sublime and the beautiful, are directly applied to the mental and emotional development of the child. Judgment and reasoning are naturally awarded the highest place in the scale of faculties. The capacity to reason refers ultimately to the facts of experience which in turn depend on a careful foundation of sense training. As Rousseau advised, young children should begin with simple exercises that will enable them to judge distances and weights and make comparisons based on the senses of feeling and sight. Later, more complex experiments will improve judgment of causation and lead the child to express himself in concrete language.

In the concluding chapter of *Practical Education* the authors observe that "all the purposes of practical education tend to one distinct object; to render our pupils good and wise, that they may enjoy the greatest possible share of happiness at present and in future."[5] The characteristic features of their system are directed toward this end: the attempt to adapt both the curriculum and methods of teaching to the needs of the child; the endeavor to explain moral habits and the learning process through associationism; and most important, the effort to entrust the child with responsibility for his own mental culture. The final goal is prudence, an "enlarged comprehensive wisdom" compounded of judgment and resolution. When the individual has cultivated the powers of reasoning, applied them to conduct, and associated them with habits of action, he is free to act in consequence of his judgment. This ideal of the independent man, able to live happily in a world of sustained moral choices, recurs frequently in Maria's fiction. And while we may not always share the authors' optimism about the all-powerful influence of education, it would be difficult to quarrel with their belief that the capacity to feel happiness resides ultimately within the individual.

The Parent's Assistant (1796)

The stories of *The Parent's Assistant*[6] established Maria Edgeworth as the leading writer for children of her day. The collection published in 1796 contained eight stories and a play, most of which were written during the family's residence at Clifton between 1791 and 1793.[7] A new edition, published in 1800, added seven new stories and a play.[8] In writing these stories, the author was motivated by a twofold purpose: to provide entertainment for her growing audience of young brothers and sisters (generally ranging in age between nine and fourteen) who served as her critics; and to demonstrate her father's educational principles in *Practical Education*. The educational theses, then, are clearly outlined in her father's prefaces: "Lazy Lawrence," for example, points out the evils of laziness and the rewards of exertion, while "The False Key" illustrates the dangers of associating with poorly educated servants. Such narrowly restrictive purposes are hardly enough to support F. J. Harvey Darton's judgment of Maria Edgeworth as "the best, perhaps, of all writers for children"[9] or of P. H. Newby's belief that in her "tales for children we meet the first living and breathing children in English literature since Shakespeare."[10] Nor would they support other twentieth-century writers' praise of her "dramatic realism," her well-sustained plots, and her skillful descriptions of character.[11] For this reason, her contributions to children's literature can best be understood within the larger history of the nursery library.

Until the latter half of the eighteenth century, very few books other than textbooks and books on courtesy had been written especially for the young. For entertainment, they shared in much of the literature designed for their elders—translations from Latin classics, tales of King Arthur, legends, ballads, lives of the saints, Aesop's *Fables,* and stories of history and travel. Many of these stories appeared in the shape of broadsides and chapbooks, and aside from being badly written, their content was often coarse, and the pictures that accompanied them were little more than crude woodcuts.

In the first half of the eighteenth century, there appeared a number of compilations which professed to be for the entertainment and profit of children. The titles were designed to attract young readers, but the contents must often have proved disappointing and depressing. James Janeway's *A Token for Children* was perhaps the most widely read, but it and other typical works of the period have been described as "grim products," conceived with a didactic and religious bias so strong that they hardly seem to us to be children's books at all.[12]

The era of "real" children's books—those created and published expressly for children—began with the establishment of John Newbery as a publisher in London in 1744. A writer, bookseller, and printer of children's books, he was receptive to new currents of thought—social, educational, and literary—and realized the potential of a literature designed especially for children. As a publisher, he improved the quality of workmanship that went into book production, popularized traditional tales in new, attractive bindings, and published several notable books (including *A Little Pretty Pocket Book* [1744] and *The History of Little Goody Two-Shoes* [1766]), written primarily to amuse children.

Nevertheless, during the Newbery era, and extending well into the nineteenth century, the general attitude toward the child remained unchanged. Parents, teachers, and theorists clung to the idea that children were miniature adults, and for this reason the values of children's books were most often adult values: virtues that adults wanted to inculcate, vices that adults wanted to condemn, and social mores that adults wanted to have imitated. The purpose was clear: to mold children from infancy or to reform them according to certain prescribed goals.

For this reason, writers for children in the late eighteenth century were generally preoccupied with didactic and religious themes and with educational theories. Aside from Maria Edgeworth, widely read authors included Sarah Trimmer (1741–1810), Thomas Day (1748–89), and Mary Beth Sherwood (1775–1851), whose books for children are fairly representative of the then-prevailing attitudes toward the treatment of children. Mrs. Trimmer typifies the explicit dogmatism, characteristic of the narrowly didactic writing of the time. Her strictures on children's books are described in her *Guardian of Education* (1802–6), in which she wrote that "there is not a species of Books for Children and Youth, any more than for those of the maturer years, which has not been made in some way or other an engine of mischief."[13] Not surprisingly, she opposed a great number of things: fic-

tion and works of the imagination, threats to the social order, cruelty
to animals, Thomas Day's dangerous philosophic notions, and Richard Lovell Edgeworth's secular approach to education. In the preface
to her best-known work, *Fabulous Histories* (1786, later known as *The
History of the Robins*), she makes it clear that her talking birds—
Dicksy, Flapsy, and Pecksy—are nothing but the creatures of a series
of fables intended to convey moral instruction to children. While the
work reflects the problems that arise among children's day-to-day experience, the lofty language and high-flown sentiments must have
unnerved, even then, all but the exceptional child.

Thomas Day's *Sanford and Merton* (1783–89) represents the type of
children's book designed to disseminate and exemplify a particular
philosophy of education. In both his life and writings, Day was an
ardent disciple of Rousseau, and in *Sanford and Merton* can be found
most of the major doctrines advocated in Rousseau's *Emile*: disdain of
the wealthy and idle; praise of the virtuous poor; simplicity in life
and behavior; fortitude in adversity; and prudence and industry. The
plot turns on the contrast between two children: Tommy Merton, son
of a rich planter and a delicate and overindulged little boy; and Harry
Sanford, a sturdy little rustic, reared according to Rousseauistic principles. Harry's superiority is constantly demonstrated, and Tommy is
counseled, directly or indirectly, to imitate him. Thus, quite unlike
the Edgeworths, Day propagates the belief that the life of the barbar-
ian is preferable to that of more civilized peoples and that, consequently, children should be educated apart from society.

Yet the affairs of the children occupy comparatively small space.
The "Infallible Tutor," Mr. Barlow, provides innumerable tales,
mostly derived from classical legends, which are intended either to
inform or to warn and reprove. Direct narrative is often interrupted
for the telling of such stories, loosely and clumsily held together by
events that concern the boys. It is not surprising that the work is
forgotten today. As Darton suggests, in "manner and form" it is now
"quite obsolete, and its lack of humor . . . will probably prevent its
ever being seriously considered again by appraisers of children's
books."[14]

Mrs. Sherwood typifies the preoccupation in children's literature
with religious teaching. The view of the child as an infant replica of
the sinful parent had, of course, informed the majority of children's
books for over a century and a half.[15] Like Janeway before her, she
writes with religious fervor, and like him, she believes that the child

is capable of understanding and correcting his fallen condition. Her widely read *The Fairchild Family* (1818–47) proposes to "show the importance and effects of a religious education," and the responsibility of educating the children is given to Mr. Fairchild, the father. His major concern is his children's natural depravity, and his great hope is that "God will give us a knowledge of the exceeding wickedness of our hearts; and we may, knowing our wretched state, look up to the dear Saviour who alone can save us from hell."[16] Mrs. Sherwood's solemn preoccupation with death and the future life can be seen in such chapter headings as "On the Formation of Sin in the Heart," "A Story on the Constant Bent of Man's Heart Toward Sin," and "A Happy Death." Occasionally, there are natural, realistic accounts of the day-to-day activities of the children, but what we (and perhaps the child reader) remember longest are the terrifying accounts of hell and damnation that attend evildoing: the coffins, vaults, and graveyards, the gibbets, corpses, and funerals.

The stories of *The Parent's Assistant* must have seemed a refreshing departure from such children's literature of the time. Unlike Mrs. Trimmer, Maria Edgeworth was not obsessed with the desire to instruct, nor did she follow Thomas Day's example as a propagandist of political and social reform. Least of all did she share Mrs. Sherwood's interest in saving souls. While her purposes are always clear, her values—thrift, self-denial, truth-telling, obedience, generosity, and thoughtfulness of others—are undeniably healthy and sound, for they teach the child to learn and grow through self-reliance. Since the stories were designed for instruction as well as amusement, the most dominant principle of plot construction is contrast: for example, the self-sacrificing Leonora versus the self-seeking Cecilia ("The Bracelets"), the humane Hardy versus the inhumane Tarlton ("Tarlton"), the generous Susan versus the selfish Barbara ("Simple Susan"). The device is most pronounced in "Waste Not, Want Not" in which both characters and situations are contrasted with symmetrical precision. Yet in the best stories, the characters are much more complex than such contrasts would suggest because of Maria Edgeworth's ability to visualize them realistically and to dramatize the conflicts between them in their social relations.

"Simple Susan" (which Scott admired) has always been one of the more popular stories of the collection—partly, no doubt, because it is told with a directness and simplicity that are pleasing to a child. The story is set in a small village near the border of Wales, and allusions to pink blossoms of hawthorn, primroses and fresh violets, and crowns of nosegays establish the freshness of a springtime atmosphere at the beginning. The plot is built largely on a conflict between a dishonest lawyer (Attorney Case) and an honest, industrious farmer (Peter Price) over a supposed flaw in Price's lease. Yet the real interest of the story centers in the children: in Barbara Case (daughter of the attorney), a conceited, ill-mannered child; in Susan Price (daughter of the farmer), a generous, sweet-tempered little girl; and in the neighborhood children who are Susan's friends. In the course of events, Susan loses her favorite pets—a guinea hen and a lamb—through the Cases' contrivances, and only near the end of the story are they restored to her. To a child, such simple events are important; but what matters historically is that this story, among others, includes elements that are relatively new in children's fiction: a plot complicated by conflicts that must be resolved during the progress of the story; suspense, important in holding a child's interest; and characters who think and talk like real ones.

"The Birth-Day Present" is another attractive story, developed largely through dialogue. The contrast between how we perceive ourselves and how others perceive us is central to the plot, and for this reason the story provides a more penetrating insight into the child's mind than many of the stories. Rosamond, the young heroine, thinks of herself as generous, and to demonstrate her generosity, she mistakenly buys a perfectly useless birthday present for her cousin. Even worse, she bestows it for the wrong reason, to reflect credit on herself. Her sister Laura, in contrast, is generally considered a miser, but in donating her half-guinea to a charitable cause, Laura proves to be more generous than Rosamond. Ostensibly, the impetuous and fallible Rosamond must learn, through trial and error, the meaning of generosity. But the story is important for other reasons as well: it is written not only for children but also from their point of view. And like "Barring Out" (in which one child convinces another that it is unreasonable to bar a headmaster from his school room) and "The Orphans" (in which children agree that a guinea must be returned to its rightful owner), it features a society of children who act and arbitrate by the rules of a child's world.

Throughout the stories, Maria Edgeworth's treatment of rewards and punishments is doubtlessly the result of her father's moderate attitudes toward punishment and his secular approach to education. Children are neither threatened nor wheedled into being good, neither terrorized nor made to feel inadequate. Often a child's recognition of having done wrong ("The Mimic," "Waste Not, Want Not") is sufficient punishment. It is usually an older child or an adult ("Tarlton," "Lazy Lawrence," "False Key") who is guilty of serious mischief such as lying, theft, or forgery. In these cases, Maria Edgeworth avoids miserable beatings and morbid deathbed repentances; banishment and imprisonment are sufficient. More typically, children are deprived of walks or playtime or pocket money. A child is rewarded more often than not by winning the goodwill of other children or the approval and respect of his elders ("The Basket Woman," "The White Pigeon," "The Mimic"). And this is as it should be since in the Edgeworths' view neither fine presents nor great rewards make children happier or better. "The happiness of childhood," they said, "peculiarly depends upon their enjoyment of *little* pleasures" (*PE,* 167).

Perhaps what distinguishes Maria Edgeworth most from other writers for children during her age is that she fully understood the nature of childhood. This does not mean that her stories are equally good. In her commitment to the development of theses, she sometimes sacrificed amusement to instruction ("Lazy Lawrence," "Waste Not, Want Not," "Forgive and Forget"). Yet at her best, she convincingly developed the tragedies and triumphs of childhood. For this reason, Annie E. Moore's estimate of her contributions still seems valid: "She set the example of a gifted writer who dignified the art of creating children's stories; broke away from most of the old traditions and made her stories stand on their own merits rather than on extraneous material; largely discarded set patterns for stories and invented interesting plots; drew a large number of fairly well-rounded child characters and developed a few unforgettable ones; wrote more fully for entertainment than any previous or contemporary writer and in so doing furnished at least two generations with good stories well suited to the time."[17]

Adolescence: *Moral Tales* (1801) and *Popular Tales* (1804)

Most of Maria Edgeworth's short stories and novelettes for adolescents are included in two collections, *Moral Tales* and *Popular Tales*.[18] On 29 January 1800 she wrote her cousin Letty that she was rework-

ing the "old stuff" not used in the children's stories: "The new stories
will begin under the title of *Moral Tales* being a new series of the
Parent's Assistant."[19] In general, the tales attempt to combine amusement with instruction in a style and subject matter suitable for teen-
agers and young adults. As fiction, the tales lack the freshness and
vitality of the children's stories since their effectiveness is often vi-
tiated by the pressure of purpose on plot and by the predictability of
the characters. Yet as Francis Jeffrey said of the *Popular Tales,* they
are "not tried by a fair standard unless the design of writing them be
kept constantly in view."[20] For this reason, the stories can best be
viewed as fictionalized treatments of the Edgeworths' ideas in *Practical Education*.

"The Good Aunt," "The Good French Governess," and "Mademoiselle Panache" each feature a model teacher, but taken together,
they provide interesting variations on the pupil-teacher relationship
and the theory and practice of learning. Mrs. Howard and her young
nephew ("The Good Aunt") demonstrate the single pupil-teacher relationship and the effectiveness of judicious home training as preparation for the public school. Madame de Rosier ("The Good French
Governess") exemplifies the role of governess within the family and
provides, as the preface points out, "a lesson to teach the art of giving
lessons." The purpose of both stories is essentially the same: to show
the importance of the teacher as adult role model and of effective
teaching methods designed to stimulate a child's curiosity and cultivate his taste for knowledge. In "Mademoiselle Panache" the theme,
that the individual is largely a product of his education, is developed
through a contrast between two families. Lady S———, preoccupied by
the artifices of fashionable society, entrusts the education of her
daughter, Lady Augusta, to the coarse Mademoiselle Panache, a former milliner. In contrast, the wise Mrs. Temple superintends the
personal growth of her daughters, Emma and Helen, early initiates in
what Richard Lovell Edgeworth called "the education of the heart"—
the development of "useful and agreeable habits, well-regulated sympathy, and benevolent affections" (*PE,* iv).

These three stories, together with "Angelina," also sketch an ideo-
logical position that is fundamental to all of Maria Edgeworth's future heroines: the belief in domestic life as a social ideal and
commitment to the rational development of the female understanding
as the surest means to happiness. "Angelina" and its companion piece
"Forester" each feature a colorful and unconventional central character

who must learn, through trial and error, the difference between illusion and reality. Freer than usual of fictionalized teaching aids, these stories typify the best of the adolescent fiction.

The liveliness and vitality of "Angelina" no doubt stem in part from its having been first constructed, like *The Absentee,* as drama and later converted into a tale. As the story opens, we see that the sixteen-year-old Anne Warwick (Angelina) is a product of an imbalanced education that cultivated literary taste over judgment. Left an orphan at fourteen, she becomes the ward of Lady Diana Chillingworth, a superficial lady of fashion. Needing escape from the follies of Lady Di and her parasitical companion Miss Burrage, Angelina reads novels from the circulating library and discovers "The Woman of Genius," written under the pseudonym Araminta. A two-year correspondence with the author induces Angelina to accept Araminta's invitation to share an idyllic existence at Angelina Bower in South Wales.

In the style of a true sentimental heroine, she sets out on a quixotic quest that leads her eventually to Araminta's comfortless cottage peopled only by a slipshod beldam and a crude Welsh servant named Betty Williams. Nurtured as she has been by Rousseau's *Eloise* and by romantic German plays, she does not see the mischief of taking on one unknown friend in her search for another. With the foolish Betty as guide, she now sets out to find Araminta in Bristol, and after a series of trying and embarrassing adventures, finally meets her sentimental friend—a stout, middle-aged woman whose coarse language and crude manners "shocked and disgusted her beyond measure."

Angelina is eventually rescued by her benevolent Aunt, Lady Frances Somerset, who tactfully points out the folly of pursuing unknown friends. Near the end, the haughty Lady Diana accidentally discovers the low birth of her deceitful companion, Hetty Burrage—"Daughter to a drysalter, niece to a cheesemonger!" Lady Frances, who now becomes Angelina's guardian, subtly emphasizes the parallel of unknown friends to her sister, Lady Diana: "If you talk of her [Angelina's] unknown friends, the world will certainly talk of yours."[21] The ending reminds us that "it is possible for a young lady of sixteen to cure herself of the affectation of sensibility, and the folly of romance" (*TN,* 1:282).

"Angelina" is generally considered an antiromance, a type of didactic fiction, popular in the late eighteenth century, in which writers sought to ridicule the prevailing vogues of sensibility and terror and addressed their mock novels to young people who were apt to be deluded by such escapist literature. The antiromances generally feature a young heroine who, stimulated by her fanciful reading, sets off on a series of farcical adventures in a desire to imitate her fictitious models. Eventually, she recognizes her folly and readjusts her mind to the real world.

Admittedly, "Angelina" burlesques the sentimental young heroine whose expectations from reading fiction are proved false by experience, but the story is not primarily an attack on sentimentalism. Maria Edgeworth's sympathies are with Angelina from the beginning. The mistakes in her education are related both to her early training (parents who failed to cultivate her judgment) and to deficiencies of her present environment. A "young woman of considerable abilities," she sees the artifice of Lady Diana's "circle of high company" and listens impatiently to her fashionable guardian's "useless lectures and reproaches." She is disgusted with Hetty Burrage, the "constant flatterer" of her guardian's "humors," and bored by the lack of stimulating books and conversation.

In her quest that follows, it is obvious that she is in search of more real and lasting goals than an idyllic life in a cottage. As she later remarks to Lady Frances, "I wished for a friend, to whom I could open my whole heart, and whom I could love and esteem" (TN, 1:274). Thus, as the preface suggests, Angelina's "romantic eccentricities" are far less important to Maria Edgeworth's purpose than "faults of a more common and despicable sort"—pride, selfishness, deceit, and coldhearted villainy. For this reason, Hetty Burrage, not Angelina, is the real antiheroine of the story. Maria Edgeworth is willing to smile sympathetically at Angelina, for romance and sentiment have temporarily misguided an otherwise amiable and docile young girl who must learn self-knowledge from the enlarged experience of living in the world. Hetty, in contrast, has denied her homely upbringing and forsaken her friends and family in an effort to gain acceptance in the fashionable world. Throughout the story, the author's sympathies are clearly on the side of the rational and well-educated or the simple and good-hearted. There is no place for a young woman compounded of pride and meanness, and for this reason Hetty is returned to her simple home at St. Augustin's Back, where she should have remained all along.

"Forester" provides a more complex variation on the learning process. Angelina's overstimulated imagination requires a cure to free her from affected sensibility and romance. This freedom restores rational balance to her mental faculties, and her independence means that she is capable of combining judgment with resolution and applying both to action. In contrast, Forester's lack of social sympathy cannot be resolved by a simple cure. The lesson that he must learn is to temper benevolence with reason through a deepening acquaintance with reality. He is not required to abandon his schemes of benevolent reform. And since moderation is the key to his change in behavior, he emerges as a more attractive thesis-oriented character than Angelina. Yet the story is less subtle and more doctrinaire than its counterpart.

The nineteen-year-old Forester, like his real-life model Thomas Day, "scorns the common forms and dependencies of civilized society." He is torn between his disdain for the indolent wealthy and his sympathy for the poor and downtrodden. Following his father's death, he is sent to Edinburgh to live with his appointed guardian, Dr. Campbell (modeled after the Scottish philosopher Dugald Stewart). Here he is exposed to two contrasted patterns of behavior. Henry, the Campbells' son, is a product of his father's belief that "education, in the enlarged sense of the word, creates the difference between individuals more than riches or poverty." Archibald MacKenzie, a relation of Mrs. Campbell and a visitor in the household, is the outcome of his mother's myopic vision that success depends on patronage and fashionable connections. These contrasts focus interest on the main character. We see that Forester is imprudent because of misguided idealism; Archibald is imprudent because he is insolent, extravagant, and deceitful. On the other hand, Henry Campbell shares Forester's love of independence, but he is also sociable and ready to sympathize with his friends in pleasure and distress. He represents the ideal of wise moderation, of true independence, to which Forester later aspires.

Forester's education in the school of common sense begins only after he leaves Dr. Campbell's household. His apprenticeship as a gardener forces him to make the first revaluation of his assumptions when his benevolent feelings for the poor and his arcadian notions about the simple life are directly countered by the ignorant insolence of an illiterate employer and his cross, ugly daughter. His first discovery, then, is that liberty of mind and freedom of opinion exist most fully in a cultivated society. As a clerk to a brewer, he learns another important lesson in social intercourse. The young men in the brewery are parasites of a mercantile system that encourages petty gain by circumventing the establishment. Forester is told that he must cooperate in the preparations for the brewery supervisor's visit, but he is unwilling to join in a scheme to defraud the firm's records to meet the supervisor's criteria. He perceives that such practices are corrupt, and in rejecting them makes a choice that is clearly rational. His learning process is still far from complete, for he yearns alternately for an arcadian life on a shipwrecked island and for a life of active benevolence. As a printer's assistant, he envisions a noble employment of "disseminating knowledge over the universe," an idealistic disguise for the reality he must discover. He is reintroduced to a circle of well-bred people but comes to see that even cultivated society is not exempt from illiberal prejudice. The young radical, Tom Random, speaks in florid prose of candor and liberality, of freedom of opinion and universal toleration. Yet the young man cannot brook disagreement with his own opinions. Forester clearly perceives that Henry Campbell's essay on reforming abuses is superior to Tom's. Henry has shown himself "the friend of rational liberty" while Tom is prejudiced and partisan. And since Forester is convinced by reason, he is fully initiated in a course of behavior that leads to independence and self-sufficiency.

"Angelina" and "Forester" are both serious studies about conflicts in social behavior, about choices between illusion and reality. "Forester" makes explicit Maria Edgeworth's views about the individual's role in society and the nature of the social order. When Forester is mistakenly suspected of theft, he reflects "that an individual in society who has friends, an established character, and a *home,* is in a more desirable situation than an unconnected being, who has no one to answer for his conduct." This is Maria Edgeworth's personal ideal, the happy home as the only reasonable alternative to society with its artificial display and merciless competitiveness. If the individual's role is relative to family, the family is also qualified by the social order of the Augustan age. As a printer's assistant Forester is also permitted to write occasional essays for the public papers. In an effort to resolve his stoical doubts about the advantages of "civilized society," he solicits public response as to what should constitute distinguishing characteristics of the higher classes in society. Henry Campbell's published reply is weighted with the voice of authority: "Those arguments in favour of subordination in society, in favour of agreeable manners and attention to the feelings of others . . . struck Forester with all the force of conviction; and he wondered how it had happened that he never before perceived them to be conclusive" (*TN*, 1:78). Like Jane Austen, Maria Edgeworth believed that class distinctions were a fact—and for the most part, a neutral fact—about society. Throughout most of her fiction, social well-being, not a change in social station, is the reward for proper conduct. But behind this apparent acceptance of the social order is her belief that a person can become what he wishes through education. In acquiring judgment (the highest of the mental faculties), he has the power and freedom to select.

As Richard Lovell Edgeworth's prefaces made clear, the *Moral Tales* and *Popular Tales* were to be interpreted within the context of *Practical Education* just as the later *Tales of Fashionable Life* were to be read as extensions of *Professional Education*. A correlation of theory with practice shows that the scheme did not always work as precisely as intended. *Practical Education*, for example, stressed the close supervision of a child's formative years: "What we are when we are twenty depends on what we were when we were ten years old" (*PE*, 315). Yet Angelina and Forester are among the first of a large gallery of characters who do not fit this prescription. Lady Frances Somerset and Dr. Campbell, the rational guardians, are not instrumental to behavioral changes since both young people learn their lessons from experience during early maturity.

The *Popular Tales* also contain a number of similar departures from theory, characters who succeed in spite of negligent early training or who fail despite positive supervision. Marvel ("The Will") is quick-tempered and impulsive but develops on his own initiative a character that is stable and prudent. Leonard Ludgate ("Out of Debt, Out of Danger") defies his rational father's advice about prudence and economy and is ruined by extravagance and crime. Caesar ("The Grateful Negro") is motivated less by reason than by impulse; his master's kindness inspires a linked human response—first gratitude, then sympathy, then loyalty, and finally duty in saving his master from armed conspiracy. In the fiction for adults, characters are often quite careless about how they have been taught and reared. Almeria ("Almeria"), for instance, goes astray despite the constructive influence of her childhood friends, and the children of Mrs. Beaumont ("Manoeuvring") and Mrs. Somers ("Emilie de Coulanges") are sensible and levelheaded despite scheming and temperamental parents.

If, in the Edgeworths' thinking, neither ideas nor moral principles are innate, what motivates prudence in the absence of carefully formed associations of learning? *Practical Education* provides the best clue: the ability to reason rests solely on the facts of the individual's experience. In associative learning, exclusion is as important as inclusion. Maria Edgeworth's villains are often guilty of lying, deceit, indolence, extravagance, fraud, and crime—vices that form no part of the experience of her model characters. Life is not, of course, so neatly organized by theory, and if the fictional characters do not always fit the theory, they do coincide with the Edgeworths' more flexible personal outlook.

Richard Lovell Edgeworth viewed life as a process of continued growth and change and measured happiness according to the individual's capacity to improve through learning. Like the leading educators of his time, he could not explain the principles of heredity. In his later years he saw that complexities of human behavior, such as resolution, could not be defined by educational assumptions. Maria, on the other hand, found it difficult to reconcile her liking for the natural and her preference for the exemplary; her most interesting heroines, like herself, are a combination of heart and head, a cross between the ancient Griselda and her own high-spirited Rosamond, with whom she compared herself. If her major characters are not always patterns of virtue and vice, her fiction, in spite of divergence from theory, is much better for it. We can assume that she made allowance for inherited good dispositions and the general influence of cultured society, as well.

The *Popular Tales* (1804), like the later *Comic Dramas* (1817), were written for the middle and lower classes, and most of the stories pit young men against commercial society in which economic security is a prime aim.[22] As the author intended, the stories are studies of conduct, explorations of rational and irrational behavior either determined in advance by educational conditioning or based on the individual's capacity to learn from experience and his freedom to choose. In theme and style they are often little more than variations of the children's stories. For example, "The Will," with its emphasis on thrift and economy, is an extension of the earlier "Waste Not, Want Not," while "Limerick Gloves," a study of party prejudice, is an enlargement of the same theme in "Forgive and Forget."

Most of the *Popular Tales,* like the children's stories, are organized on the principle of contrast: two nephews ("The Will," "The Manufacturers"); two brothers ("Murad the Unlucky"); two planters ("The Grateful Negro"); two families ("The Contrast"). The purpose throughout is generally the same: to demonstrate the rewards of virtue (industry, economy, generosity, honesty) and the evils of vice (idleness, dissipation, and crime). Because of this didactic preoccupation, the stories are now less interesting as fiction than as useful documentaries of eighteenth-century middle-class life. And here their historical importance is obvious. They stand apart from the current fiction of the time by treating the average middle-class man and woman with dignity and respect.

Maria Edgeworth and William Wordsworth, were, in fact, responding to the same impulse: to choose "incidents and situations from common life" and to bring "language near to the language of men." Young men are miners and manufacturers, shopkeepers, tradesmen, and farmers who make decisions about jobs, money, and marriage. Young women are mothers, wives, and daughters; but they are also governesses, caretakers, or co-partners with their husbands in business. For this reason, they receive no special treatment. Social and economic goals reflect the ethical discrepancies of Maria Edgeworth's time: the acquisition or loss, the use and abuse of fortune are at once a key to character and an index to social relationships.

The *Moral Tales* and *Popular Tales* reflect conventional attitudes toward fiction of their age, when "the business of fable was to illustrate moral truth; it was an *exemplum* anchored to a text, and like all *exempla*, exhibited in its perfection that system of punishments that we call poetic justice."[23] The technical imperfections of the stories are no doubt a reflection of this thinking. Yet they are remarkably modern in what they have to say. The willingness of heroes and heroines to make judgments independent of social convention stems from the Edgeworths' faith in the development of a rational, lucid intellect as the surest guide to happiness. In novels like *Harrington, Patronage, Helen, Ennui, The Absentee,* and *Ormond,* Maria Edgeworth develops—perhaps for the first time in fiction—a serious connection between the individual's private and public responsibility. But in the short tales of her early career, the belief that the individual's most important duty is to the self—to seek and gain moral independence that leads to responsible and enlightened behavior—seemed a relevant enough thesis to teach adolescents.

Chapter Three
The Education of the Heart

We are better for knowing that when Maria Edgeworth's *Letters for Literary Ladies* appeared in 1795, women in England had plenty of sermons and conduct books to help them understand what was required of them. The social conventions of the age dictated that woman's role was to love and obey parents and husbands, to love and rear children in the way they should go, and to exercise justice toward servants (if there were servants). Such conduct books as Fordyce's *Sermons to Young Women* and Gregory's *A Father's Legacy to His Daughters* (the most famous guidebook of its kind during the eighteenth century) warned women of the example of Eve and advised them to be on guard against their love of gossip and slander and their tendency toward suspicion, jealousy, affectation, and frivolity. A woman was urged to be chaste, modest, and retiring, yet her rewards were most often given in the form of admiration for beauty unaccompanied by such virtues. She was expected to be strong-minded enough to resist importunate pleas of a lover, yet submissive enough not to exert her personality against her husband. Her blessings were most often found in the joys of love and motherhood or in the rewards of a life devoted to family and community.

Her narrowly prescribed public role, on the other hand, was dictated by the age. In the late eighteenth-century, women were without any direct political or economic power, and for all practical purposes they were minors in the eyes of the law. Any money they might inherit or earn by their own efforts became part of a joint matrimonial or family estate unless otherwise secured to them by special allowance or settlement. It was impossible for a woman to obtain a divorce before 1857 except by an act of Parliament. Married women spent many years in child-bearing, and their life expectancy was not long; the high rate of infant mortality was also a constant source of sorrow. The ordinary middle-class woman's education was largely confined to the three *R*'s or to accomplishments such as drawing, music, painting, and needlework. Religious and moral instruction was generally taken care of by attendance at church and by parental guidance.

Significantly, it was at this time that women writers began to be concerned about the poor quality of education available to girls and to produce books to improve their education. Mary Wollstonecraft was, of course, a pioneer, for it was she—more than any other woman of her age—who recognized the economic injustices suffered by women: the limited opportunities for employment, the low wages of governesses, and the wife's loss of property rights. But other female writers as different as Hester Chapone, Jane West, and Hannah More at least shared the belief that good would follow from the improved education of women. The time was not yet right for any real efforts toward vocational training for women or for thinking them capable of filling responsible leadership roles in society. It is not surprising, then, that most conduct books of the period and most fiction written by women should be concerned with the twofold education of the heart (politeness, accomplishments, government of the temper and affections) and head (generally devoted to the female's reading, with special warnings against sentimental novels).

It is important to recognize that part of Maria Edgeworth's mind was on the side of benevolence and feeling and that the heart mattered to her as much as the head. "Some people have a notion that the understanding and the *heart* are not to be educated at the same time," she wrote in *Practical Education;* "but the very reverse of this is, perhaps, true; neither can be brought to any perfection, unless both are cultivated together" (*PE,* 182). It is worth remembering that her father always thought her heart better than her head[1] and that he judged her major character defect as "an inordinate desire to be beloved." Maria Edgeworth the writer was committed both to a rational, secular system of morality and a feeling for life, and no single formula can explain the subtleties and ambiguities of her fiction. Like Jane Austen, she saw the late eighteenth-century novel of sensibility—with its stress on the quantity and violence of emotion exhibited—as a gross debasement of the Shaftesburian "moral sense," the ethical faculty that spontaneously led the individual to fulfill the law of his being in exercising the social virtues and benevolent emotions. Yet social sympathy and good feelings were inadequate bases for moral judgments, uneducated by reason. Maria Edgeworth thought that women and men should be equal and that only a planned program of education could prevent women from becoming the slaves of men or of fashion and custom.

Her career began with *Letters for Literary Ladies*, a short part-fictional, part-essay work concerned with the education of women. The fiction of the middle years of her career (ca. 1802–8) was designed primarily for an audience of females and written at a time when her Aunt Ruxton was a more important literary influence than her father. *Helen*, the one novel written after her father's death, is the fullest expression of her own views, the most intensely feminine of all the fiction about women. By grouping the fiction designed for females, we preserve rather than disrupt continuity; all of the works are set in England and in all of them the women have more to do than the men. Since the heroines (e.g., in *Belinda* and *Leonora*) are not always themselves the center of interest, we must find the general pattern of values in the novels as a whole. In spite of technical imperfections, the works designed for women are fascinating for what they have to say; in all of them, Maria Edgeworth attempts to reconcile the claims of the head and the heart, and indeed makes that conflict a central issue in the novels.

Letters for Literary Ladies (1795)

Letters for Literary Ladies, in three parts, opens with "Letter From a Gentleman to His Friend Upon the Birth of a Daughter" and with an "Answer to the Preceding Letter." The two letters are based on the author's memory of a correspondence between her father and his friend Thomas Day on the subject of female authorship. Day, who felt that a woman should live in seclusion from society and under the unqualified control of her husband, had strongly disapproved of Maria's efforts to become a writer. When the publication of her translation of *Adèle et Théodore* (1783) was prevented by Thomas Holcroft's published translation, Day sent Edgeworth a congratulatory letter that contained an "eloquent philippic" against female authorship. Edgeworth responded by defending the cause of female literature; and although he disagreed with Day about the role of women and the propriety of female authorship, his respect for his friend's views kept Maria from publishing until after Day's death in 1789.

The two letters are argumentative essays that debate the issue of higher education for women. The "Gentleman" (representing Thomas Day's views) sets up the premises for rational debate by presenting all of the cherished stereotypes about women. Females are by nature inferior, the argument begins. Women have less knowledge than men because their dissipation of time and their domestic duties prevent them from applying themselves to more serious public issues. They cannot be trusted with political power since they rarely permit reason to govern their conduct. And because they have "more susceptibility of temper, and less strength of mind" than men, they are naturally more inconsistent in behavior. The dangers attendant to successful female authorship are especially foreboding. Literary ladies want to display their abilities, and in so doing they excite the envy of their own sex without fear of consequences. They also endanger their chances for matrimony, since by feeling equal to or superior to men they become "losers in love as well as in friendship." The "Gentleman" implies that woman's exclusion, by custom or law, from public and private institutions of learning is the real reason for her subjugation; but his concern is with the effect rather than the cause. It is unlikely that a sex prone to prejudice, inconsistent behavior, and thirst for applause will better themselves or society by literary success. Subordination of the sex is thus the wisest course.

"Answer to the Preceding Letter" (representing Richard Lovell Edgeworth's views) is an eloquent argument for sexual equality based on reason. Education is not only essential to a woman's personal happiness, the "Answer" argues, but to the mutual enlightenment of both sexes. In marriage an educated woman is able to live with her husband as a friend and converse with him as an equal. In motherhood a woman who instructs herself is better able to instruct her children. Yet the major thrust of the "Answer" is not directed toward preparing a woman for either marriage or motherhood. The value of a woman's abilities and acquirements must be judged "by the degree in which they contribute to her happiness" (*TN*, 8:441). The way to happiness begins with self-knowledge and hence to self-approval. Three years later (in *Practical Education*, 1798), Edgeworth reaffirmed many of these same beliefs. His protest against half-instruction in favor of a wider curriculum (that included the modern sciences and stressed modern as opposed to classical education) shows that he had much more in mind than simply literary education for women. Accomplishments (a subject that also preoccupied Fanny Burney and

Jane Austen) are bad only when abused—when skills in music, dancing, and drawing are used as matters of competition or exhibition, or
as a deliberate means of attracting male admiration.

"Letters of Julia and Caroline," the second part of *Letters for Literary Ladies,* is a fictionalized correspondence between two young
women, the one representing sense (rational discretion and prudence),
the other sensibility (overrefined emotion and excessive susceptibility). Julia, the sentimentalist, clearly embodies the catalog of faults
that the "Gentleman" expressed to his friend. The rational center of
the correspondence is Caroline, for six of the seven letters are written
by her. Since Julia's behavioral ethic is geared to feeling, it is not
surprising that over a period of several years she should separate from
her husband, engage in extramarital affairs, and later die in ignominy
and shame. As we shall see from *Leonora,* Maria Edgeworth was not
comfortable with the epistolary form, and "Letters of Julia and Caroline" reflect the insecurities of an author who is unable to use the
form to dramatize character and advance action. Caroline's letters, especially, tend to collapse into discursive monologues on the subject
of female behavior. Nevertheless, the correspondence between the
young women contributes two themes that are important to the later
works: the belief in moderation, the coexistence of feeling and reason;
and the worth and value of the individual.

The most important letter is the fifth, in which Caroline recalls
Julia's major intellectual error in a conversation during their last
visit: "You asked 'of what use philosophy could be to beings who had
no free will, and how the ideas of just punishment and involuntary
crime could be reconciled?' " (*TN,* 8:479–80). Julia's belief that
man's actions are involuntary is based on the popular metaphysic that
belief is something felt by the mind and not the result of a rational
process. It is the right doctrine to flatter emotional temperaments—
and to encourage belief that the individual's control over his own destiny is so limited that the "conduct of that little animated atom, that
inconsiderable part *self,* must be too insignificant to fix or merit attention." Caroline's response places the emphasis where Maria Edgeworth wants it: "I believe I answered, 'that it might be *nothing*
compared to the great *whole,* but it was *every thing* to the individual' "
(*TN,* 8:480). The author's ideal is not a romantic glorification of the
self; but the values that she admires—the worth of discriminating
analysis by the conscious mind, the full exertion of individual personality, and the importance of the individual within "one vast whole"—

had more in common with the thinking of her Romantic contemporaries than she realized.

"An Essay on the Noble Science of Self-Justification," the third part of *Letters for Literary Ladies,* is the best selection of the group because of an almost perfectly controlled contrast between the author's attitude and what is actually stated. The essay advises females on the surest means of winning an argument with males; a few techniques, if used skillfully, can become powerful defensive weapons in battles of verbal repartee. Almost any topic can become a subject for debate—the use of time, matters of taste and opinion, and personal habits. Weak and timid females who lack talent are qualified by nature for self-justification. They can assume a kind of blameless innocence and humility. And there is always the weapon of silence, if rightly timed, so that the provoker will think himself stupid instead of the accused. The "Essay" is characterized by many of the traits of Maria Edgeworth's best style—unity, humor, wit, and simple elegance. At her Aunt Mary Sneyd's suggestion, she used the "Essay" as a foundation for *The Modern Griselda,* a brilliant short novel about the failure of a marriage.

The Modern Griselda (1805)

In November 1803 Maria wrote Sophy of her plan "to put the precepts in the Essay on self-justification in practice upon husbands of various characters. . . . I mean to allow my modern Griselda three husbands, a moderate allowance, for the full exercise of her talents—."[2] As it turns out, Griselda has one husband, and the novella is better for it. It allows the author to focus directly on the heroine, to develop her through a succession of related incidents, and to realize her most fully in the cumulative effect of her behavioral pattern. Griselda Bolingbroke and her husband have been married a few short weeks, but long before the happy event Griselda has decided to subdue her husband by female power. She is equipped with all of the mannerisms of heroines in sentimental novels—headaches, the charms of beauty heightened by anguished sensibility, magic smiles, vacillating tones of behavior. Sometimes she is sullen, sometimes "radiant with joy." The slightest offense or trivial remark is sufficient reason for battle or tears. She is armed with the stock theories of sentimental heroines: passion is more important than friendship in marriage, and true love means total agreement on all subjects.

It is natural that Griselda should seek the friendship of Mrs. Nettleby since she too is involved in subduing a husband, an "obstinate fool." The two women devise a malicious plan to prove that the newly married Mrs. Granby is "Nothing—absolutely nothing; a cipher; a nonentity." The following week Mr. Bolingbroke will entertain with a reading from Chaucer's Griselda. Mrs. Granby is certain to approve of Chaucer's pattern wife, an attitude so outdated that she can be made an object of ridicule by the ladies of the party. As it turns out, Griselda is mortified that Emma Granby's gracious feminine manner and enlightened and tolerant views about women disrupt her plan. After attempting a number of theatrical roles, with all the skill of a bad actress, Griselda seizes the part of submissive and dutiful wife. Finding her in this role, her husband persuades her to accompany him into the country to spend a few weeks with the Granbys. It is here that the final drama is played out. Persuaded until the last that she will conquer, Griselda delivers her climactic line with daring: "I have reflected sufficiently . . . and decide, Mr. Bolingbroke—to part" (TN, 6:462). As the carriage waits at the door, Griselda has her "One word more" and blames her husband for his own weak self-indulgence.

Maria Edgeworth wrote her publisher, Rowland Hunter, that her father "*liked* Griselda as to style I think better than almost anything I have written."[3] Her father's preference is entirely justified, for Griselda Bolingbroke is one of her most brilliant fashionable heroines. The earlier "Essay on the Noble Science of Self-Justification" developed an idea while "Griselda" dramatizes a situation based on the idea. It is less an exploration of mind than a dramatization of behavior through dialogue. The story begins almost accidentally: "Is not this ode set to music, my dear Griselda?" said the happy bridegroom to his bride. "Yes, surely my dear: did you never hear it?" (TN, 6:409). At her husband's request, Griselda plays the ode on her harp. Bolingbroke tells here that the ode is "charming" and asks her to play it again. The words are now slightly altered. "This time he omitted the word '*charming*'—she missed it, and, pouting prettily, said, 'I never can play any thing so well the second time as the first' " (TN, 6:409). The story runs from "he omitted the word" to the fatal "one word more," from comic absurdity to the absurdly tragic, the story of a dialogue destroyed.

The conflicts between Griselda and her husband are developed largely through a series of trivial disputes that steadily accentuate the growing tensions in their relationship. For example, if he is late for dinner, she reproaches him for being "always late." His pronunciation of a word provokes a heated debate about the use of language, as prescribed by prevailing taste and authority. In general, "When he wanted to read, she suddenly wished to walk; when he wished to walk, she was immersed in her studies. When he was busy, she was talkative; when he was eager to hear her converse, she was inclined to be silent" (*TN,* 6:419). In one instance, "Just before the birth of their child, which, by-the-bye, was born dead, a dispute arose between the husband and wife concerning public and private education" (*TN,* 6:418). The dead child, mentioned almost as a parenthesis, is less important than a trifling dispute, a major issue in the evolving situation of a disintegrating marriage.

Marriage is, above all, a situation in which people must deal with reality, and the three married couples in "Griselda" succeed or fail in terms of their perception of truth. Mr. Nettleby believes, according to his wife, that "women were born to obey, and promised it in church." Yet we see him only through the impressions of his feather-headed wife, an unreliable yet transparent witness. His refusal to befriend the newly separated Griselda and to "meddle" in the marital difficulties of others aligns him in the cause of good sense and right thinking. The Nettlebys' husband-dominated marriage is less than felicitous; yet Mr. Nettleby, in perceiving the truth of his wife's character, acts from the force of his own convictions. The Granby and Bolingbroke marriages suggest the primary thesis of the story, that if we cannot live with ourselves, we cannot live with others. Emma Granby would not have made the promise exacted from the ancient Griselda, for she could never have respected a man who required such a promise. Long before her marriage, she had learned the value of self-knowledge, the truth of self-discovery that means the difference between freedom and slavery. In control of herself, she has no need to master others. The puzzled Griselda asks Emma how she exercises power over her husband. "By not desiring it, I believe . . . I have never used any other art" (*TN,* 6:454).

The Bolingbroke marriage demonstrates the hopelessness of a relationship based solely on passion. Because of her inordinate love of dominion, Griselda has failed to cultivate "well-regulated sympathy," essential to the education of the heart. Since she does not know herself, she cannot understand or judge others. And the reader understands this, without the Granby marriage as contrast, because Maria

Edgeworth clearly dramatizes her characters in their social and domestic relationships. As the Bolingbroke marriage becomes "a perpetual scene of disputes and reproaches," the author lets us see for ourselves how their quarrels "grew more bitter, and the reconciliations less sweet." Griselda makes herself ridiculous by playing a role; Bolingbroke is not conscious that he has any part to perform. The author could feel safe in leaving the ending to the reader's imagination.

Belinda (1801)

Belinda, Maria Edgeworth's first full-length novel, employs the theme of a young girl's entry upon life, the well-established format of Fanny Burney's *Evelina* (1778) and *Camilla* (1796). The plot relies heavily on the experiences of Richard Lovell Edgeworth's youth, his acquaintance with the life and death of Sir Frances Delaval, and Thomas Day's experiment with Rousseau's child-rearing principles. In fitting these to the Burney format, Maria Edgeworth produced a highly complicated novel of manners that added Jane Austen to her admirers. The novel makes a penetrating study of love, courtship, marriage, family, and friendship. But more importantly, it dramatizes the conflicts within Maria Edgeworth's own personality and environment, conflicts between reason and feeling, restraint and individual freedom, society and the free spirit.

As the novel opens, Mrs. Stanhope has succeeded in fastening Belinda Portman, her one remaining unmarried niece, to the fashionable Lady Delacour for a winter season in London. Belinda soon discovers that Lady Delacour's dazzling wit and charm are only a facade that masks the pain and agony of her approaching death. In a lengthy flashback, Lady Delacour reveals the truth of her dissipated life: her hatred of her gambler-sot husband; her failure as a mother; and her betrayal in friendship by the dissolute Harriot Freke. Her greatest fear is that she is slowly dying of breast cancer, caused by the recoil of a pistol which she once used in an aborted duel with another woman. The friendship between Belinda and Lady Delacour dominates the first half of the novel until Lady Delacour is convinced that Belinda, too, is a deceiver, scheming to marry Lord Delacour after her death in hopes of becoming a fashionable viscountess.

After the confrontation scene—the most brilliant of its kind in Maria Edgeworth's fiction—Belinda goes to reside with the rational

Percival family, an idealized picture of domestic happiness and tranquillity. The Percival household is consciously inserted as part of Belinda's learning process, yet she does not remain here long. When Lady Delacour decides to submit to an examination by a competent doctor, Belinda agrees to return to the Delacours and accompany the family on their visit to the surgeon. As it turns out, Lady Delacour's malady is not incurable, and her recovery, the author tells us, is gradual and complete.

Since the original sketch of *Belinda* included Lady Delacour's death, critics have generally viewed her recovery as anticlimatic since much of the drawn-out conclusion must disentangle Clarence Hervey (Belinda's principal suitor) from his wearisome wife-training experiment. Yet to see the novel only from this view obscures the value that Maria Edgeworth places on Lady Delacour's wit and intelligence. In the early chapters she may be viewed as an object of pity since her suffering stems from conflicts within herself. Yet throughout the novel, and especially after her reformation, she is used as the author's principal means of assessing the conflicting claims of sense (represented by the rational Belinda and Lady Anne Percival) and sensibility (represented by the irrational Miss Moreton and the simple-minded Virginia). Maria Edgeworth's sympathy is ostensibly with Belinda, but running counter to this is her obvious admiration for Lady Delacour's candor and vitality. In this subtle countermovement of the plot, Lady Delacour expresses the author's qualified disapproval of Belinda, at the same time that she reconciles passion and reason, affection and esteem, nature and art—a balance essential to the education of the heart.

Lady Delacour's complexity, the contrast between her own perceptions of reality and illusion and the reader's apprehension of her, is skillfully developed through images of the theater. Her highly polished diction and verbal manipulation, her assumption of theatrical roles, her dramatic ridicule of her fashionable acquaintances are part of the mask which she presents to the world. For this reason, her intimate confession of her past indiscretions to Belinda becomes a symbolic prelude to the novel, for it signifies Lady Delacour's acceptance of Belinda as sole friend and confidante. The values of this acceptance and the dimensions of the friendship between the two become the controlling interest of the plot, both before and after Lady Delacour's reformation.

For Lady Delacour, true friendship means artlessness (as opposed to

artifice), sincerity, and honesty. Although she misjudged these qualities in Harriot Freke, she believes that Belinda embodies them. Motivated by the dictates of her heart (not head) and imagination (not
reason), she entrusts Belinda with the secrets of her past and with the
innermost recesses of her thinking. It is significant that Lady Delacour drops the dramatic pose only with Belinda; yet because of her
youthful inexperience and untried innocence, Belinda neither fully
understands Lady Delacour's worldly wisdom nor does she accept her
as a model and guide. She sees from Lady Delacour's example that
the life of a fine lady does not lead to happiness. And she disapproves
of Lady Delacour's ceremonious civility toward her husband and her
daughter. Admittedly, Belinda learns to judge from experience, but
her judgments are primarily reflective. As a character, then, she is
little more than an abstract embodiment of principles—"goodness itself, and gentleness, and prudence personified."

Principles are the basis of Belinda's virtuous resistance to temptation—the temptation to follow her misguided aunt's advice, for example, or to accept the marriage proposal of the foppish Sir Philip
Baddely, or to encourage the attractive Clarence Hervey who she believes is engaged to another. Yet Lady Delacour is suspicious of rigid
principles and sees in Belinda's extreme prudence an unnatural behavior pattern founded on artfulness and deceit. Since Lady Delacour neither respects nor loves her husband, her tense confrontation with
Belinda has little to do with the jealousy of love. The "writhings of
the heart, the agony of a generous soul" are a sign, not of madness,
but of a total commitment of affection. The lesson that Lady Delacour attempts to teach Belinda, here and elsewhere, is that friendship
and love involve commitment. Lady Delacour makes the point most
forcefully in her revealing monologue preceding the confrontation:
"For what was Harriot Freke in comparison with Belinda Portman?
Harriot Freke, even whilst she diverted me most, I half despised. But
Belinda!—Oh, Belinda! how entirely have I loved—trusted—admired—adored—respected—revered you!" (*TN*, 3:175).

The Percival household, where Belinda resides after leaving the
Delacours, is an oasis of harmony and tranquillity. Here she meets
Mr. Vincent, Mr. Percival's ward, who in time becomes her suitor.
Here she also comes face to face with the boorish Harriot Freke whose
theories about the rights of woman and female delicacy are countered
by Mr. Percival's judgments about prudence and the influence of
public opinion. The Percivals are little more than didactic abstrac-

tions, but their principles are crucial to the countermovement of events that follows after Belinda returns to the Delacours. Advising Belinda on matters of the heart, Lady Anne says that happiness comes from discovering the real character of another and that this is best accomplished in private society, preferably in domestic life. As we acquire knowledge of the good qualities of others, their persons become agreeable when we become *accustomed* to them. In the same somber manner, Mr. Percival reasons on the dangers of first loves. Young people generally form their first notions of love from poetry and romance and afterward transfer the images to the first objects they behold; the attraction is thus not based on esteem, but on illusion and fancy.

Belinda's return to the Delacours coincides with the beginning of Lady Delacour's reformation. It is important to see that Lady Delacour's narrative voice continues to express Maria Edgeworth's presiding vision, for Lady Delacour "Reformed" does not differ markedly from Lady Delacour "Unreformed." With a touch of the theater, she herself decides how she will appear in her new character. She imagines herself the "subject of witticisms, epigrams, caricatures without end" and prefers to leave the fashionable world in "voluntary retirement" rather than in "forced retreat." After she discovers that she does not have cancer, she is even more decisive about the conduct of her future behavior: "A tame Lady Delacour would be a sorry animal, not worth looking at. Were she even to become domesticated, she would fare the worse" (*TN*, 3:306). It would be unthinkable, she tells her husband, for Lady Delacour to "wash off her rouge, and lay aside her air, and be as gentle, good, and kind as Belinda Portman" (*TN*, 3:306). Lady Delacour Reformed does not mean that she is less perceptive of truth or less aware of circumstances—the truth of her husband's inferior intelligence, for example, or the awareness of Belinda's unnatural reserve. Lady Delacour Reformed and Lady Delacour Unreformed pursue the same object: to educate Belinda in the affections of the heart.

To accomplish this objective, Lady Delacour pits "Love and I" against "Lady Percival and Reason" and cautions Belinda that she cannot live all her life "in this heavy armour of reason." In a crucial discussion on the subject, Lady Delacour tells Belinda that a "heart such as yours is formed for love in its highest, purest, happiest state" (*TN*, 3:330). Belinda volunteers such terms as "sense" and "virtue" and argues that esteem is the foundation of love. Lady Delacour reminds her that "we often see people working at the foundation all their lives without getting any farther" (*TN*, 3:330). When Belinda alludes to Mr. Vincent's "solid good qualities," Lady Delacour asserts that "we never fall in love with good qualities, except, indeed, when they are joined to an aquiline nose. . . . I am more afraid of it than of all his solid good qualities" (*TN*, 3:330). If Belinda cannot decide by "solid good qualities," then by what must she be determined? And Lady Delacour gives her the key: "By your heart, my dear; by your heart: trust your heart only" (*TN*, 3:331).

Belinda expresses esteem and gratitude for Vincent, but not love. As it turns out Vincent is an unworthy suitor after all because of his addiction to gambling, and Lady Delacour does not miss the opportunity to turn the Percy principles to her advantage. Mr. Percy's theories about first loves are equally applicable to the second; and Mrs. Percy's approval of Vincent is a wrong judgment, rendered by a reasonable pattern lady, a model of behavior that Lady Delacour has rejected for herself. Before the discovery of Vincent's treachery, Lady Delacour also deflates the Percival notion, real or imagined, about the impropriety of leading a suitor on: "Let things have gone ever so far, they can stop, and turn about again" (*TN*, 3:349).

Maria Edgeworth never liked Belinda. After reading Mrs. Inchbald's *The Simple Story*, she wrote to her cousin Sophy, "I really was so provoked with the cold tameness of that stick or stone Belinda, that I could have torn the pages to pieces: and really, I have not the heart or the patience to *correct* her. As the hackney coachman said, 'Mend *you*! better make a new one.' "[4] The author's language is echoed in Lady Delacour's disapproval. Lady Delacour fears that Belinda will despair of winning Clarence Hervey because of his "mistress in the wood" and will marry "some stick of a rival, purely to provoke him." Belinda hopes, in reply, that she will never "marry *a stick*." Lady Delacour effortlessly scores the point: "I am convinced you never will—but one is apt to judge of others by one's self" (*TN*, 3:265). Lady Delacour expresses the author's views most forcibly in the final chapters. "Have you a heart?" she asks Belinda. "And it can exist without love?" (*TN*, 3:440). In the closing scenes the author reintroduces the properties of the theater so that Delacour functions both as character and critic. After Clarence Hervey realizes the failure of his wife-training experiment (Virginia feels gratitude, not love), he is ready to declare his passionate attachment to Belinda.

Lady Delacour points out that Belinda has for months seen all his merits "with perfect insensibility" and despite her efforts remained "stone blind" to his love. "—Let us now see *Belinda in love,* if that be possible" (*TN,* 3:456). Maria Edgeworth's refreshing ending satirizes not only the stock devices of the novel of sensibility but the behavior of her subdued heroine and the tame advice of the Percivals as well. When Belinda suggests that novelists err "in hurrying things toward the conclusion," Lady Delacour retorts, "That's right, my dear Belinda; true to your principles to the last gasp. Fear nothing—you shall have *time* enough to become accustomed to Clarence" (*TN,* 3:462). In the concluding tableau Lady Delacour subtly counterposes the "rules" of art with the "laws" of probability: "Clarence, you have a right to Belinda's hand, and may kiss it too: nay, Miss Portman, it is the rule of the stage" (*TN,* 3:463).

It would be useless to argue that the novel is not greatly flawed by an overcrowded plot and by inconsistencies in character and theme. The author herself admitted that in the Hervey-Virginia experiment her attempt to join truth and fiction did not succeed, since the contrast between the fictional Hervey and the real-life Thomas Day was much too pronounced. The point she wants to make with it is, of course, clear. Clarence places himself in the category of those who learn from experience. Yet he sees that his own experience is based on an educational experiment, that his feelings confute his system, and that his principles do not necessarily mean happiness. Virginia's inability to distinguish between the value of diamond earrings and a moss rosebud teach him that innocence cannot be equated with ignorance. He also comes to see that he nearly sacrificed his entire happiness to a sense of duty. Yet the author wants us to equate duty with honor since Hervey saves Vincent, his rival suitor, from suicide.

The three suitors who present themselves to Belinda are obviously intended as instructive antitheses. Sir Philip Baddely, the foolish baronet, is pure caricature. Mr. Vincent voices the Edgeworth's disapproval of moral instinct as a guide to conduct, for his feelings are "always more powerful than his reason." Clarence Hervey's behavior is inconsistent (on three different occasions he considers avowing his passion for Belinda before he is disencumbered from Virginia), yet he is not an abstraction. He is less attractive as the suitor of Belinda than as the friend of Lady Delacour, with whom he is aligned from the beginning. In selecting Belinda over Virginia, he chooses reason over sentiment, a choice consistent with the theme of the novel, if Belinda is considered the heroine.

Marilyn Butler suggests that "the theme of the novel is precisely the opposite of *Camilla*'s: instead of learning to submit to authority, Belinda learns to escape it, and to rely instead on her own judgment."[5] Admittedly, Belinda learns prudence through reflection, but she fails to learn emotional commitment through sympathetic identification with others. The "education of the heart" includes prudence, esteem, and reason, but it does not deny affection, vitality, and imagination. Neither in the adolescent nor in the adult fiction does Maria Edgeworth condemn feeling. Feeling and reason are both necessary for moral judgments, and both must be practiced in moderation.

It is obvious that Belinda Portman's flaw is excessive prudence, an error of the heart, not of the head. She does little more than personify unnatural reserve and cautious restraint, and Lady Delacour's dominating presence registers Maria Edgeworth's own disapproval. In spite of the cumbersome plot, the novel succeeds because of Lady Delacour, the only character whose thoughts and actions are consistently dramatized in the course of the action. Her personality combines intellectual and intuitive brilliance in such a way that no other character (and no reader) is untouched by her. Early in the novel, she expresses her outlook on life: "Life is a tragicomedy! Though the critics will allow of no such thing in their books, it is a true representation of what passes in the world" (*TN*, 3:51). Her unique modernity is that she never quite represents an affirmation of human happiness—only an acceptance of the human condition, of the world as it is. It would be difficult, even today, to disagree with Walter Allen's judgment of her as "one of the great achievements in English fiction."[6]

Leonora (1806)

In conception and design, *Leonora* appears as a strange interlude between *Belinda* and the shorter heroine-dominated stories of *Tales of Fashionable Life*. In part, the novel was Maria Edgeworth's answer to Madame de Stael's *Delphine,* which appeared two months after the Edgeworths' arrival in Paris in October 1802. In sympathizing with extramarital passion and thereby flaunting subjective authority as a guide to conduct, *Delphine* had enraged public opinion at the time of publication. Perhaps Abraham Niclas Clewberg Edelcrantz, who proposed to Maria on 3 December 1802, shared in the negative critical response. She must have thought so, for after the family returned home she began *Leonora* as an answer to *Delphine*. But her real motive was to please Edelcrantz. Madame de Stael might write authoritatively about *affaires de coeur*, but Maria Edgeworth's personal experience hardly qualified her for a story of sexual passion, intrigue, and jealousy. In November 1803 she wrote Sophy of her determination to "set about *Leonora* & to read the *Sorrows of Werther* in their black binding" as preparation for "the genuine sentimental style."[7] Like *Werther*, *Delphine*, and *La Nouvelle Héloïse*, *Leonora* involves a triangle of lovers. And like *Delphine* and countless other novels of the sentimental school, *Leonora* is a novel in letters, Maria's only use of the form after the brief "Letters of Julia and Caroline."

A summary quickly suggests the author's departures from her literary models. Leonora and Mr. L—— have been happily married for eighteen months when Leonora's friend Olivia accepts an invitation for an extended visit to L—— Castle. Olivia is, in short, a composite portrait of the sentimental heroine. She finds escape from "commonplace morality" in metaphysics and German novels. She defies the "absurd bandages of custom" by separating from her husband and acquiring a lover. She is injured by scandal because of "a fatal mixture of masculine independence of spirit, and of female tenderness of heart." And she asks Leonora to "counsel," "guide," and "save" her. It is a large request for one so unpracticed in wordly experience as Leonora. Like Belinda she believes that matters of the heart are based on esteem; yet her cautious adherence to principles—prudence, fortitude, duty, respect for the rights of others—causes her to misjudge the character of Olivia and almost costs her her marriage.

Olivia begins her affair with Mr. L—— innocently enough. Simple curiosity motivates her to test Leonora's temper, and although she would not deliberately destroy her friend's happiness or peace of mind, she easily enough succumbs to her passion for L——. Each of the lovers manufactures reasons for continuing the affair. The sophisticated, urbane Gabrielle, Olivia's confidante and the story's most memorable character, encourages Olivia's belief in the moral sense. After all, since Olivia loves L—— against her will, she cannot reproach herself for "involuntary injustice" to Lady Leonora. Olivia proposes that the moral sense "resides primarily and principally in the nerves, and varies with their variations," a humorous burlesque of the sentimentalists' tendency to link ethics to feelings and feelings to social behavior. Olivia is convinced that Leonora has never known the passion of love and for this reason remains blind to whatever passes before her eyes. Thus it is Olivia's *duty* and *virtue* to deceive, since Leonora will remain happy as long as she is ignorant. Mr. L———'s justification for the liaison is much more serious: "Lady Leonora is calm, serene, perfectly sweet-tempered, without jealousy and without suspicion; in one word, without love" (*TN,* 8:338). He sees in Leonora's cold, insensitive behavior only a proof of conjugal affection and believes that Olivia, in contrast, is capable of feeling genuine passion.

The two lovers are about to leave for Russia when a packet of Leonora's letters (sent by her mother) arrives and convinces L——— of his injustice in mistaking his wife's demeanor. The story might have ended here with a graceful reconciliation between husband and wife and with Mr. L———'s ready acknowledgment of the valuable lesson he has learned from experience. As it is, the plot labors and turns around a series of improbable catastrophes. The most serious obstacle to interpretation is that Mr. L———'s return to his wife is not self-motivated. After proclaiming his "undivided love" for Leonora (she has nursed him through a near-fatal illness), he declares his intention to sail as planned. At this point a friend of Leonora's sends a packet of Olivia's revealing letters which Leonora resists opening from a sense of honor. The same correspondent also describes the content of the packet in a letter to Mr. L———, and a mutual friend of the reunited couple writes that Lady Olivia, "thus unmasked by her own hand has fled to the continent, declaring that she will never more return to England."

The novel would have been better without the unmasking. Richard Lovell Edgeworth's own succinct judgments of the novel are still the best. He thought the novel failed because it had "no story, to interest the curiosity; no comic, to make the reader laugh; nor tragic, to make him cry."[8] Part of the problem is that the epistolary form is not congenial to what Maria Edgeworth can do best: develop character through scenic groupings and natural, spontaneous dialogue. Her personal letters of 1804 refer frequently to her anxieties about the novel. Her major mechanical difficulty was how to extricate Mr. L——— honorably from his commitment to Olivia and thus achieve a happy ending. And although her father provided a detailed solution which she greatly modified before the book was published, this did little to remedy unusually thin characterization and lack of action.

The "moral" of the story depends on how we interpret the ambiguous denouement. Butler believes that "the central crux of the plot becomes the process by which Mr. L——— makes up his mind between his mistress and his wife."⁹ According to this view, the rational mind must necessarily perceive the differences in value between a Leonora and an Olivia and wisely choose the wife over the mistress. Hawthorne, on the other hand, sees Leonora as the center of the novel's action; ostensibly, the heroine's rationalism wins her husband back but in the process her rational faith leads only to misery.¹⁰ That the plot supports both interpretations dramatizes the failure to provide a controling center for the action.

A comparison of *Leonora* with *Belinda* suggests yet another possibility. The heroes of both novels are first misled by passion and then by duty. Since the idea of duty was central to nineteenth-century culture, the willingness of a fictional hero to sacrifice happiness to duty may not have seemed puzzling to a nineteenth-century audience. In both novels, duty is equated with honor in an effort to make the heroes' actions seem probable, yet the plots of both labor to extricate the young men from their untimely predicaments. Both novels feature colorless young women who suffer from excessive prudence. Yet because of the use that Maria Edgeworth makes of Lady Delacour's brilliant intelligence, the countermovement in *Belinda,* as we have seen, suggests a disapproval of unnatural prudence and affirms the necessity of emotion and feeling.

Leonora allows for a similar interpretation, for the heroine does not reject feeling. Her friendship with Olivia is precipitated more by an affectionate heart than by a reasonable head. Olivia's betrayal teaches her, painful though the experience is, that a "sense of duty and of general benevolence" does not in itself lead to happiness. In one of her most revealing letters, she explains the changes that have come about in her marriage. Since she once possessed her husband's love (including passion), she cannot now be content with friendship. Having known his ardent affection as a lover, she cannot be happy with esteem. Later when her rational mother, the duchess, counsels "dignified silence" Leonora rejects the advice as the "superstition of prudence." Her most decisive action follows her open discovery of the affair. It is important to see that Leonora's denunciation of Olivia is Maria Edgeworth's exposure of false sensibility. Olivia's attachment to Mr. L—— is based on dishonest emotion and selfishness, the ultimate debasement of the moral sense. The culprit is not Mr. L——, a passionate man temporarily deluded by imagination, but Olivia, a victim of excessive sensibility.

Since Mr. L—— is generally characterized with sympathetic detachment, his views of marriage are also important to the counter-movement of the plot. His strongest criticism of female virtue is directed at the pattern wife whose observances of duty merely protect her own reputation among family and friends. Love involves more than the trappings of establishment and social approval. As Mr. L—— expresses it, "I do not desire to be loved well enough for a husband; I desire to be loved sufficiently for a lover" (TN, 8:337). He views his wife's behavior as a pattern of "duty-work kindness" and interprets her unnatural reserve as a lack of affection. Leonora refuses the temptation to test her husband's jealousy even though she is presented with an attractive opportunity; but this does little more than confirm her husband's belief that if he and his mistress remained in Russia for ten years, Leonora would "conduct herself with the most edifying propriety." Leonora's sprightly friend Helen suggests what Maria Edgeworth herself must have believed: "I think that I could not have resisted the temptation of coquetting a little—a very little—just to revive the passion of the man whom I really loved" (TN, 8:347). Even the duchess, sagest of counselors, finally advises her daughter not to indulge too strongly her taste for retirement or for the exclusive society of intimate friends.

The views of Leonora and Mr. L—— together suggest that something besides esteem is necessary for a happy, stable marriage. Leonora's major problem is that while she understands and even admits the importance of feeling, her behavior, like Belinda's, is confined largely to a reflection on principles. Mr. L—— seems justified in expecting tangible proof of his wife's affection; yet in his resolute allegiance to duty, he is equally ensnared by principles. Since the denouement does not accomplish a satisfactory compromise between the principles of Leonora and her husband, we must find the theme in the general pattern of values in the novel as a whole.

Olivia is almost pure caricature, less interesting in contrast with her rival, Leonora, than in comparison with her friend, Madame de P——. Olivia freely abandons herself to careless passion while Madame de P——, detached and worldly wise, stresses the utility of passion as an instrument of power. Olivia might begin with innocent intentions, but she ends as coldhearted and selfish as her friend—and it is clear that Maria Edgeworth disapproves of both. The duchess, Leonora's mother, and General B, Mr. L——'s confidential friend, function as voices of rational authority; yet Leonora learns primarily through reflective experience and Mr. L—— hardly learns at all.

Helen's point of view speaks for the livelier, more intuitive strain of female personality, a humanized balance of sense and sensibility. For this reason, she is the only character capable of making moral discriminations, of seeing the disparity between proper norms of conduct and the actualities of human behavior. Her role in the novel is limited. Yet her criticisms of Olivia's sentimental absurdities and Leonora's cautious restraint sound clearly through the countermovement of the plot. If we accept Helen's views in the spirit that the author offers them—as a valid compromise of extremes—then the novel is neither an unqualified condemnation of affection and feeling nor a wholehearted acceptance of esteem and reason. *Leonora*, like *Belinda*, makes the case for moderation.

Manoeuvring (1809)

The enthusiastic response to *Belinda*, especially among the people who mattered to Maria Edgeworth, might have encouraged her to duplicate its format. *Patronage*, her longest novel, was still to come, yet she did not intentionally write another three-volume novel. In *Moral Tales* and *Popular Tales*, she had established a format that best suited her purpose, the short or medium-length tale, comparable in length to a long short story or novella. Except for *Patronage* (initially intended as a tale), *Belinda*, and *Leonora*, the bulk of Maria Edgeworth's fiction for adults was published as "tales." The reason, of course, is clear when we remember that "novel" meant something quite specific to Maria Edgeworth and her reading public.

The causes for the disrepute into which the novel had fallen after the age of Richardson and Fielding have been carefully examined by historians of the novel. It will suffice here to point out that Maria Edgeworth and her father fully subscribed to the popular belief in the pernicious moral influence of novel reading. Their major target was sentimental novels that Clara Reeve, their contemporary, described as "a great number of whining, maudlin stories . . . calculated to excite a kind of morbid sensibility, which is to faint under every ideal distress, and every fantastical trial."[11] *Practical Education* makes clear that the Edgeworths shared with their contemporaries the belief that reading exercised marked influence on the development of character. Readers, especially young women, might seek to emulate the corrupt behavior of fictional heroines and end up as deluded victims of disordered imaginations.

Maria Edgeworth was not alone in her hesitancy to accept the role of novelist. In 1796, when *Camilla* was ready for publication, Fanny Burney regretted having to call the work "a novel." Five years later, in her advertisement to *Belinda,* Maria Edgeworth decisively rejected the term: "The following work is offered to the public as a Moral Tale—the author not wishing to acknowledge a novel." Jane Austen poked gentle fun at the squeamishness of both her contemporaries and in so doing immortalized them in her famous defense of novel reading in *Northanger Abbey.* In Maria Edgeworth's thinking, "Tale" avoided the stigma then attached to the novel, but beyond this simple convenience she did not attach any special literary significance to the "tale." She preferred *Modern Sketches,* Mrs. Ruxton's suggestion, "a thousand times better than 'Fashionable or Unfashionable Tales.' "12 In 1809, she wrote to her cousin Margaret, "the title to be *Moral Stories*—as *Moral Tales* we have used already. . . ."13 Her references are to the first and second series of *Tales of Fashionable Life,* the title under which the fiction following *Leonora* was published.

Almeria, Mme de Fleury, Manoeuvring, and *Emilie de Coulanges,* all short tales of fashionable life, were conceived as early as 1802–3 when the author still thought of her reading public as being largely female. As expected, then, she reexamines in these tales the issues she thought most important to female conduct and happiness: the values of real friendship; the bases of happy courtship and marriage; the pleasures of domestic and the evils of fashionable life; and above all, the importance of intellectual and moral education in the shaping of character.

Manoeuvring is the best of the four tales, for in it the author returned to the format that had served her so well in *The Modern Griselda* and *Belinda,* an enlargement of the comic sketch that explores in full one or two major characters. Mrs. Ruxton, who was always partial to her niece's polished, sophisticated heroines, preferred *Manoeuvring* to *Ennui.*14 And Richard Lovell Edgeworth thought that *Vivian* would stand "next to Mrs. Beaumont & Ennui. . . ."15 That the author generally referred to *Manoeuvring* as "Mrs. Beaumont" suggests a concentrated emphasis on dramatizing her heroine rather than exploring the dimensions of a thesis. The story does have an obvious point to make—that Mrs. Beaumont's behavior is not a pattern for imitation—but the other characters recognize her for what she is long before the story is ended. And in the best scenes she is treated with comic detachment so that we see in her transparency the amusing difference between reality and delusion.

As the story opens, Mrs. Eugenia Beaumont is well entrenched in an intricate triple scheme to acquire fortune and power: she hopes to prevent the aged Mr. Palmer, a wealthy West Indian planter and friend of her deceased husband, from meeting the sensible Walsingham neighbors whose good character and conduct might encourage him to divide his wealth; she aspires to marry her own daughter Amelia to the deceitful, middle-aged Sir John Hunter, heir apparent to the large Wigram estate; and she plans to marry her son Edward to the immature Albina Hunter, Sir John's half sister, for her large, independent fortune. The plot takes on the dimensions of formal farce, as Mrs. Beaumont gradually becomes trapped in the web of her own self-generated entanglements. Yet none of the schemes works according to plan. Her children, who prefer to marry into the Walsingham family, resolutely refuse to marry the Hunters; and to save face, Mrs. Beaumont ends up marrying Sir John herself, only to discover to her mortification that he is disinherited. Mr. Palmer, whose intelligence Mrs. Beaumont misconstrues as naive simple-heartedness, detects the heroine's deceit in spite of her artful secrecy. And Albina, the most manageable of all silly creatures, delivers the final blow by marrying Lightbody, Sir John's waiting man, thereby destroying Mrs. Beaumont's final plan to absorb Albina's fortune by marrying her to a nephew.

As in *The Modern Griselda* and *Belinda,* the action of *Manoeúvring* is found in the dialogue. Mrs. Beaumont's speech is the language of disclosure, and since she is developed consistently, we can rely on her talk as measurement of her character and personality. After sending Albina off with a message to her brother, Mrs. Beaumont speaks to her son Edward in an attempt to establish in his mind a connection between Albina's departure and Mr. Palmer's forthcoming visit. Edward begins the conversation:

"But, madam, were you not saying something to me about Miss Hunter?"

"Was I?—Oh, I was merely going to say, that I was sorry you did not know she was going this morning, that you might have taken leave of her, poor thing!"

"Take leave of her! ma'am: I bowed to her, and wished her a good morning. . . . Surely no greater leave-taking was requisite, when I am to see the lady again to-morrow, I presume."

"That is not quite so certain as she thinks, poor soul! I told her I would send for her again to-morrow, just to keep up her spirits at leaving me. . . .

I say I am not so sure that it would be prudent to have her here so much, especially whilst Mr. Palmer is with us, you know. . . ."

"You know, Edward, my dear, you know?"

"I don't know, indeed, ma'am."

"You don't know!"

"Faith, not I, ma'am. I don't know, for the soul of me, what Mr. Palmer's coming has to do with Miss Hunter's going." (*TN*, 5:23)

Mrs. Beaumont hopes that Edward is interested in Albina and attempts through manipulated verbal probing to judge his feelings for her. Her scheme is to pity Albina (using pathetic epithets) and suggest Mr. Palmer's likely disapproval of Albina, hoping that Edward will come to her defense. Since this ploy fails, Mrs. Beaumont tries a new strategy: she approves of Miss Walsingham, Edward's own choice, and then attempts to discredit her on the basis of her intellectual superiority. This plan also fails, but it prepares the way for the open confrontation in which Edward forces his mother into her one moment of truth. He makes her see the sincerity of his attachment to Marianne Walsingham and the impossibility of his marrying Albina Hunter, a young woman "wishing to be married," but "not capable of love."

Even when Mrs. Beaumont's plans should succeed—when others are enlisted in the dirty work—the scheme fails because the calculations are rooted only in the framework of her deluded thinking. It is a delightful moment when Dr. Wheeler, carefully briefed in his strategy, counsels Mr. Palmer against the cold English climate. After being habituated to hot Jamaican weather, he must surely "fall a victim to the sudden tension of the lax fibres." This verdict is just enough to convince Palmer not to extend his visit beyond the scheduled week. But Mrs. Beaumont, assuming that Wheeler will take the cue, protests fashionably against this "cruel, cruel decree." Dr. Wheeler "apprehended that he had misunderstood Mrs. Beaumont's note, and he now prepared to make his way round again through the solids and the fluids, and the whole nervous system, till, by favour of *idiosyncrasy,* he hoped to get out of his difficulty, and to allow Mr. Palmer to remain on British ground" (*TN*, 5:41). Mrs. Beaumont conciliates the doctor with a handsome tip and another invitation to breakfast. But she does not extricate herself quite so agreeably from Albina Hunter, who, like the other objects of Mrs. Beaumont's design, is not what she seems.

The repeated pattern of epithets—"dearest Miss Hunter," "my darling," "my dear," "my love," "my dear child," "affectionate girl"—creates a tone of condescension that defines Mrs. Beaumont's real opinion of Albina, that she has little understanding and, consequently, has too little capacity to deceive her. Since Albina is a simpleton, she reasons, it is safe to disclose to her all the strategies of the master plan, underestimating the influence of her own example as a mistress of intrigue. There is wonderful irony in the scene where Mrs. Beaumont pits Miss Walsingham against Miss Hunter on the subject of literature, assured that the Walsingham intelligence will frighten Edward away from the object of his affection. Albina, primed by Mrs. Beaumont not to show too much learning, overplays the role and inevitably exposes her vulgarity: "She could give no opinion of any book—oh, she would not give any judgment for the whole world! She did not think herself qualified to speak, even if she had read the book, which indeed she had not, for, really, she never read—she was not a *reading lady*" (*TN*, 5:71).

If Mrs. Beaumont is to free Amelia from commitment to Sir John Hunter, the only way to acquire his expected inheritance is to marry him herself. Albina must, of course, be manipulated in the proper way to accomplish the happy alliance. Mrs. Beaumont's language is again punctuated by epithets—"dear little saucy creature," "dear mad creature," "dear headstrong creature," "dear innocent little creature"—half teasing, half patronizing, appropriate to the object in view. The scheme might go off well if "dear innocent" Albina had not learned to dupe her mistress, a lesson she was not intended to learn. Her language even takes on the social polish of her mistress, so that her contrasting verbal styles gauge the progress of her wordly knowledge. In the undeceiving scene Mrs. Beaumont explains, with proper sighs and tonal embellishments, that Edward is engaged to Miss Walsingham. Albina, by now fully educated in the game, almost forgets to make the appropriate response. Remembering her own and her brother's best interests, she reacts "with intermitting sighs, and in a voice which her position or her sobs rendered scarcely audible, talked of dying, and of never marrying any other man upon earth" (*TN*, 5:142).

The story begins with a carriage ride, hurrying Albina away to do Mrs. Beaumont's bidding. The story ends with another carriage ride, but this time the passengers are quite different. Seated bravely by her new spendthrift husband, Mrs. Beaumont—now Lady Hunter—

waves to her family, and as the horses drive off in the distance, the story moves full circle. The details of the plot that we might wish away would have seemed important to Maria Edgeworth. The background of Sir John Hunter's disinheritance—the rightful heir to the Wigram estate is a Spanish nun, rescued by Captain Walsingham and aided by him in the restoration of her property—allows Walsingham to prove his courage and thereby merit Amelia's hand. Yet the real center of interest is not plot, but character, the subtle motives that shape actions and interactions of human behavior. Mrs. Beaumont, like Lady Clonbrony in *The Absentee,* is only required to reveal herself. And in her process of self-exposure she fully justifies the reasons for her being.

Helen (1834)

We have earlier alluded to the seventeen-year literary silence that followed the publication of *Harrington* and *Ormond* in 1817. After her father's death in the same year, Maria Edgeworth completed and published his *Memoirs* (1820) because he had asked her to. But her real incentive for writing was gone. Her father had served as her major literary editor and adviser—indeed, as her partner. And now that she lacked his guidance and support, she was afraid "to venture what had not his corrections and his sanction."[16]

Helen, the novel with which she finally broke her long silence, proved to be exceptionally difficult to write, not only because of the "absence of the strong mind and tender care of her father,"[17] but also because she consciously sought to make departures from her earlier writing practices. In the first place, she wanted to avoid overt didacticism: "I have been reproached for making *my moral* in some stories too prominent— I am sensible of the inconvenience of this both to the reader & writer & have taken much pains to avoid it in Helen. . . ."[18] Brevity, too, was important, a lesson she had learned from the long-winded *Patronage.* In fact, she was disappointed that *Helen* would be published in three volumes instead of two, but assured her sister Honora that there was no padding: "Far from having stretched a single page or a single sentence to *make out* a third volume, I have cut as much as ever I could—cut it to the quick."[19] In addition, she wanted to minimize the crowded fashionable scenes that had so preoccupied her in the earlier stories. And while such scenes do occur in

Helen, they are subordinated to the more realistic rendering of domestic life and manners among the Whig aristocracy.

In keeping with the author's intention, *Helen* is less a development of theme or purpose or moral than an exploration of character; and instead of manipulating characters, like so many puppets, to meet the needs of plot or purpose, the author now arranges situations in which characters can reveal themselves for better or worse. The first volume establishes the domestic interrelationships of the principal characters: Helen Stanley, an orphan now living with the local vicar and his wife; Helen's best friend, Cecilia Davenant, recently married to General Clarendon; Lady Davenant, Cecilia's mother; Granville Beauclerc, the son of Lady Davenant's deceased first love, and the ward of General Clarendon; and Horace Churchill, a guest of the Clarendons.

The first volume moves slowly, at first, as the characters are gradually revealed through talk among themselves. Helen accepts Cecilia's invitation to reside at Clarendon Park, an English country manor and the setting for most of the novel's action; Lady Davenant tells Helen the story of General Clarendon and Cecilia's courtship and marriage and observes that a Colonel D'Aubigny was one of Cecilia's former suitors. Cecilia lies to her mother and husband about a childhood promise to Helen and later misleads Helen into thinking that Beauclerc is engaged. In a lengthy flashback, Lady Davenant relates her life history to Helen. Beauclerc arrives at Clarendon Park and involves his guardian in a heated dispute over his wish to make a sizeable loan to a thriftless friend. Then follows a family discussion about great and small people (including a disproportionate tribute to Scott) and two fashionable parties that combine "aristocracy of birth and talents."

Such slender threads of action do not appear promising. In fact, many of the events in the first two volumes seem only a postponement of the serious action. Yet Maria Edgeworth's express purpose is to win respect for her characters. And since all of them are flawed by nature or experience, they suggest—more than in any of the other fashionable tales—the complexity of reality as it is. For this reason, Lady Davenant, whose position in public and private life forms the basis for the novel's social and aesthetic judgments, provides the key: "We must take people as they are; you may graft a rose upon an oak, but those who have tried the experiment tell us the graft will last but a short time, and the operation ends in the destruction of both" (*TN,*

10:51). Taking "people as they are" means that the author now views her characters as mixed products of circumstances that are partly external and partly within themselves.

Lady Davenant is an impressive achievement, combining good taste, good breeding, sense, and feeling with a remarkably astute intellect; yet neither she nor her marriage is perfect. In her youth her idol was sacrificing herself for others. During her early marriage, she attempted to subdue her husband through power and provocation, but learned through experience that differences must be solved through mutual tolerance, generosity, and forgiveness. Her neglect of her daughter's education is her greatest failure, a mistake that she freely admits: at the end, she tells Cecilia, "The fault was mine, the suffering has been yours" (*TN,* 10:451).

General Clarendon, a man of discipline and common sense, has " 'made up his fagot of opinions,' and would not let one be drawn out for examination, lest he should loosen the bundle" (*TN,* 10:110). It is easy to dislike the brusque general and his sister Esther, a plain outspoken young woman. Yet the passion of both for truth is justified in the evolving pattern of the plot. Clarendon realizes that public and private reputation cannot be separated and when, in the past, private intrigue, scandal, and suicide in his own family became public, he resolved against marriage. Cecilia, of course, changes his mind toward marriage but not toward principle: that love and honor are inseparable. His later inquiry about Cecilia's past attachments has less to do with her romantic involvement than with the truth and openness of her character. Her failure to understand this and his failure to make her see it eventually lead to tragedy.

But what appears in Clarendon's character as obstinacy or rigid adherence to principle becomes, in fact, an unquestioned commitment of self to love, marriage, and friendship. And the "whole line of the great and masculine virtues," as Lady Davenant calls them—constancy, fidelity, fortitude, magnanimity—are realized in the private drama of the third volume. Esther Clarendon resembles her brother in tone and style of speech and in brusqueness of manner. But what finally matters is that the forthright manner of both brother and sister is matched by tenderness of heart and sympathetic identification with others. It is Esther Clarendon who finally befriends Helen in spite of censure by capricious public opinion. And it is she again who embraces the repentant Cecilia as a sister, "separation or not."

Beauclerc is always "ingeniously wrong," yet "his good habits, and

good natural disposition held fast and stood him in stead" (*TN,*
10:112). Although the author regretted that he sank into a "mere
lover," he provides a useful contrast with his guardian and with the
less attractive Horace Churchill; and his perfectly absurd insistence
on saving the worthless Beltravers from financial ruin becomes a
dramatization of learning through experience. The author's treatment
of the Beauclerc-Beltravers relationship shows how carefully she
avoided object lessons, for her point is neither retributive justice nor
enlightened self-interest. Beauclerc lavishes "tens of thousands" of
dollars on Beltravers' estate; in return, Beltravers encumbers the entire investment with gambling debts and later attempts to smear the
reputation of Helen Stanley, his sister's successful rival for Beauclerc's
affection.

Helen, brought up in luxury and trained in fashionable accomplishments, is the opposite of what she might have become—a
wholly natural and unaffected young woman, gifted with a warm,
sympathetic heart and generous affections. Yet she is vulnerable. Her
"inordinate desire to be loved" means that she "determined to become all that she was believed to be." She does not, like Belinda,
remain a passive observer of the scene; commitment to others involves
full participation in the emotional experience of life, and her learning
is realized through living. Instead of condemning her imprudent and
extravagant uncle—as earlier heroines would surely have done—she
recalls him for his love and affection, a legacy of the heart that has
inspired in her the principles of duty and truth as well as generosity.

Cecilia is an attractive, vivacious young woman, so anxious to
please her mother and husband that she fears displeasing them. She
chooses for a husband a man who very much resembles her mother,
and she holds both of them in awe. It is easy to blame her for her
endless falsehoods, yet to view her only as the chief sinner is to mis-
read the novel as Maria Edgeworth herself interpreted it.[20] The moral
that truth is preferable to falsehood is subordinate to the novel's
larger accomplishment, the close examination of human motives. Cecilia is motivated by good intentions, and if she practices deceit, her
mother and husband must be held partly responsible.

The novel's continuing examination of human conduct and character shifts from a domestic to a public setting in the two parties that
close the first volume and the social scenes that dominate the earlier
chapters of the second. These settings provide the author with a particularly fruitful opportunity to focus upon character as it is revealed

through dialogue. In such settings the public personas that people adopt complicate the perception of true character. And so Helen is given an opportunity to judge the young men around her by their words. As Lady Davenant remarks, "There are few actions and many words in life; and if women would avail themselves of their daily, hourly, opportunities of judging people by their words, they would get at the natural characters" (*TN*, 10:144). The boring Henry Churchill—admittedly, overdrawn for the requirements of his role—shows that egotistical self-love and fashionable delusions are as common to men as to women; but he also enables Helen to test her perceptions of character. With Helen, the reader comes to see through Churchill's conversation that he seeks to "excite general admiration." He ridicules departing guests, displays uncommonly bad taste on literary subjects, and paces through a variety of affected conversational styles and unsuccessful poses—"unsuited to the manly character!—so Helen thought, and so every woman thinks." A hawking expedition allows Helen further opportunity to compare Churchill with Beauclerc, but her decided negative judgment of Churchill is formed when he admits an instance of plagiarism.

In the second volume, two events are developed at length: the fashionable party that includes the sisters Lady Katrine Hawksby and Lady Louisa Castlefort as guests, and the political dinner that Cecilia sponsors on her mother's behalf. Both increase Helen's knowledge about society, and both suggest that people are what "nature, education, and circumstances have made them" (*TN*, 10:250). Lady Katrine and Lady Louisa have "no head" to hide their "want of heart." Lady Katrine, a sarcastic, pretentious spinster, "naturally hates every body that is going to be married." Her sister, in contrast, has married "a little deformed man" for establishment: family title, equipages, magnificent houses in town and country. Both young women are victimized partly by character flaws and partly by the influence of a marriage-minded society. Lady Davenant makes the point to Helen: "Every girl in these days is early impressed with the idea that she must be married, that she cannot be happy unmarried . . . it requires some strength of mind to be superior to such a foolish, vain, and vulgar belief" (*TN*, 10:182).

Strength of mind is as necessary to woman in her public as in her private domestic relationships, and the political dinner that Cecilia sponsors shows that it is pointless not to take people as they are. Lady Cecilia hopes to foster good will between her mother and Ladies

Masham and Bearcroft, two influential women whom Lady Davenant has affronted. The conversation fares badly in mixed company, worse when the ladies are alone. Lady Bearcroft, "out of her place in society, and without any fault of her own," repels others by her vulgar manners and boisterous voice: "Amazing entertaining we are! so many clever people got together, too, for what?" (*TN*, 10:235). Lady Masham slanders Lady Bearcroft after she leaves the room. Yet despite their rude manners, both women, in Lady Davenant's judgment, have "resource of heart" and "frankness of feeling." And there the matter rests. If we know ourselves, we, like Lady Davenant, see and accept people as they are.

The first two volumes of *Helen* are thus a realistic examination of character—of the casual interplay between individuals in their daily life and between the individual and society. Since "Women cannot, like men, make their characters known by public actions," they must depend upon words; and yet "how cautious we should be in deciding from appearances, or pronouncing from circumstantial evidence upon the guilt of evil design in any human creature" (*TN*, 10:268). The "look and manner, and voice and emphasis," the "pause and precipitation" may make great impressions on others in society, but how do we discern the truth of one's character, the reality behind the mask? And how do we accept human frailty and "take people as they are"? The same questions are posed in the third volume, but the focus now returns to the private lives of individuals, as the plot complications that have been slowly developing in the first two volumes build to a crescendo in the third.

Two years before her marriage to General Clarendon, Cecilia had a slight romantic involvement with Colonel Henry D'Aubigny, and during the courtship the couple exchanged a series of letters. Following D'Aubigny's death, his brother Thomas plans to publish the letters, fulfilling Henry's request for revenge on Cecilia who spurned him. The evening before the Davenants' departure for Petersburg, where Lord Davenant has accepted a diplomatic assignment, Clarendon receives a packet of Cecilia's letters from an anonymous correspondent. Since Cecilia has assured Clarendon that he was her first love, she naturally reasons that her marriage is doomed if he discovers that the letters are hers. Thinking of her mother's precarious health and her love for Clarendon, Cecilia persuades Helen to let Lady Davenant and Clarendon think that it was she—not Cecilia—who wrote the letters. Time and again, in the weeks that follow, Cecilia prom-

ises Helen that she will confess the whole story to Clarendon; but her
courage repeatedly fails her, and she is forced to manufacture lies that
involve her and the people who mean most—her mother, her husband, and her best friend—in a complicated web of deceit and
intrigue.

Meanwhile, cruel rumors begin to taint Helen's reputation and
threaten her engagement to Beauclerc. Innuendoes circulate in the
newspapers, and Cecilia and the General independently discover that
a distorted and scandalously titillating version of the correspondence
is about to be published. The General is able to stop publication, but
by now he has lost faith in Helen and retracted his original promise
to give her away at her wedding. Helen at last sees Cecilia's selfish
cowardice and falsehood and realizes that she herself has been sacrificed by an ignoble friend. Yet she has freely participated in the falsehood and instead of saving Cecilia, as Lady Davenant requested, has
only succeeded in corrupting her further.

Helen leaves the General's household and spends the next several
months with his sister, Esther, in Wales. As winter changes to
spring, she slowly recuperates from emotional exhaustion. A child is
born to Cecilia, and still she does not confess; by now, she has lost
the General's esteem and is partially estranged from him. At this
point, Lady Davenant returns home, seriously ill, and Cecilia is
moved by the gravity of her mother's illness to confess the full story
of her prevarications. Helen, finally freed from guilt, marries Beauclerc, but the reconciliation between Cecilia and Clarendon must
undergo a period of further uncertainty before Lady Davenant inter-
venes and saves the marriage.

As a sustained development of an emotional crisis, the third volume of *Helen* is superior to anything else in Maria Edgeworth's fiction. The major relationships—Cecilia and Helen, Cecilia and
General Clarendon, and Helen and the General—are subjected to increasing pressure so that the reader is irresistibly involved in both
their private experiences and complex mental states. Most of the action transpires in a series of tense, well-developed dramatic scenes
which strip bare human motive and frailty. The personal drama begins as Cecilia turns to Helen for help:

"Oh, Helen! would you make me the death of that mother?—Oh, Helen,
save her! and do what you will with me afterwards. It will be only for a few

hours—only a few hours!" repeated Lady Cecilia, seeing that these words
made a great impression upon Helen,—"Save me, Helen! save my mother."
She sank upon her knees, clasping her hands in an agony of supplication.
Helen bent down her head and was silent—she could no longer refuse.
"Then I must," said she.
"Oh, thank you! bless you!" cried Lady Cecilia in an ecstasy—"you will
take the letters?"
"Yes," Helen feebly said; "yes, since it must be so."
Cecilia embraced her, thanked her, blessed her, and hastily left the room,
but in an instant afterward she returned, and said, "One thing I forgot, and
I must tell you. Think of my forgetting it! The letters are not signed with
my real name, they are signed Emma—Henry and Emma!—Oh folly, folly!
My dear, dear friend! save me but now, and I never will be guilty of the
least deception again during my whole life; believe me, believe me! When
once my mother is safely gone I will tell Clarendon all. Look at me, dear
Helen, look at me and believe me."
And Helen looked at her, and Helen believed her. (*TN*, 10:287)

Then follows Helen's introspective examination, the first of her
searching attempts to analyze her mind and emotions:

"What am I going to do? To tell a falsehood! That cannot be right; but
in the circumstances—yet this is Cecilia's own way of palliating the fault
that her mother so fears in her—that her mother trusted to me to guard her
against; and now, already, even before Lady Davenant has left us, I am
going to assist Cecilia in deceiving her husband, and on that very dangerous
point—Colonel D'Aubigny." Lady Davenant's foreboding having already
been so far accomplished struck Helen fearfully, and her warning voice in
the dead silence of that night sounded, and her look was upon her, so
strongly, that she for an instant hid her head to get rid of her image. "But
what *can* I do? her own life is at stake! No less a motive could move me,
but this ought—must—shall decide me. Yet, if Lady Davenant were to
know it!—and I, in the last hours I have to pass with her—the last I ever
may pass with her, shall I deceive her? But it is not deceit—only prudence—
necessary prudence; what a physician would order, what even humanity requires. I am satisfied it is quite right, quite, and I will go to sleep that I
may be strong, and calm, and do it all well in the morning." (*TN*, 10:288)

Cecilia's failure to tell the truth leads to increasing constraint and
reserve in her friendship with Helen. But more noticeable is the effect
of evil on Cecilia's conscience—her real moment of self-discovery as
she changes from "generous sympathy with her friend, to agony of

fear for herself." In duping her friend Helen, she is shocked by her "own paltering manners and her friend's confiding generosity." And in her long confession to Helen, near the end, she attempts to describe her mental agony, the "dark deep-seated sorrow," the "torture of remorse" (TN, 10:427). The change in Helen is likewise admirably conceived. Her mind is weakened by anguish and self-reproach, but she finally recognizes Cecilia for what she is: "You are more to be pitied than I am; sit down, sit down beside me, my poor Cecilia; how you tremble! and yet you do not know what is coming upon you" (TN, 10:372).

A major strength of Helen is that complexities of human experience—especially, the contrast between the nature of reality and our perceptions of it—come to be understood by the characters themselves. Cecilia recognizes that all the falsehoods meant to save her mother and her marriage were in vain and that postponing her confession has intensified her own punishment. Helen is most surprised by the effect of Cecilia's confession on "characters which she thought she perfectly understood" but who now "appeared in these new circumstances, different from what she had expected." She had not anticipated Cecilia's open candor or Lady Davenant's sympathetic acceptance of Cecilia; and she had expected Clarendon to show more feeling toward his wife and less bitterness and anger over his disappointment in love.

Maria Edgeworth's experience taught her, in the years after her father's death, that people often follow ends of their own without perceiving clearly what it is that impels them. And so in Helen, she emphasizes how large a part instincts and impulses play in the lives of men and women. Despite flaws in plot construction and a didactic attitude—visible but subdued—her realistic treatment of character makes Helen the most "modern" of her fashionable tales. Truth is itself relative to character, but not more important than characters, all blessed with faults and virtues alike. At the end Lady Davenant tells Helen to be true to herself and praises her for not being too perfect. And as to her marriage to Beauclerc, "Take him, for better for worse, you must" (TN, 10:445). The advice is a fitting summation of the education of the heart.

Chapter Four
Education for Public Service

Early in 1805, Edgeworth asked Maria to put away her "pretty stories & novelettes" and turn her thoughts toward "a *useful* essay upon professional education."[1] Her "pretty stories" were tales and novels like *Belinda, The Modern Griselda,* and *Manoeuvring,* polished drawing room stories designed for a female audience and written especially to please her Aunt Ruxton. But now, in preparation for *Essays on Professional Education,* she embarked on a solid course of reading that required sustained, analytical thought. In addition, close collaboration with her father meant crystallizing his ideas about adult male issues, especially the moral and intellectual training necessary to fulfill one's private and public responsibility. In the preface to the first series of *Tales of Fashionable Life* (1809), Richard Lovell Edgeworth pointed out that "in these volumes, and in others which are to follow," his daughter's purpose was to "disseminate . . . some of the ideas" in *Essays on Professional Education* (*TN,* 4:211). This scheme did not, of course, work as precisely as intended. Yet the real significance of *Essays on Professional Education* is that Maria Edgeworth's preparation for writing it shifted her attention away from "female" concerns to "male" issues and matters of public importance. For this reason, her major novels published between *Essays on Professional Education* (1809) and her father's death in 1817 helped to establish her reputation as a serious writer for adults—not because they propagated educational theory, but because they dealt significantly with men in public life and with the larger economic, political, social, and moral issues of societies.

Essays on Professional Education (1809)

As an educational treatise, *Essays on Professional Education* is not a substantial achievement, perhaps because Richard Lovell Edgeworth considered it an "admirable vehicle for any thing we can say on any subject."[2] It lacks the empirical authority of *Practical Education* and sometimes repeats what the earlier work had said more convincingly about the psychology of childhood and learning. For this reason, the pedagogy of the book is less important than the attitudes or principal themes that underlie the work as a whole. The opening chapter explores the first major theme, that education effectively neutralizes individual differences to the extent that children can be trained for distinction in any profession. The choice of profession should be made by the parent, and professional training, through associative learning, should be commenced as early as possible, preferably in infancy.³ The chapters that follow describe what is expected of young men intended for medicine and law, for the church and military service, and for other leadership roles in private and public life. From these chapters emerge the second principal theme: the necessity of moral independence, since a man's success in public is related directly to his private character. Careers in politics and the church often depend on patronage and preferment and for this reason are perhaps less desirable than law and medicine. Ideally, the vocation of a country gentleman, one who serves as head of a household, as landlord or elected official, or simply as a good citizen provides the greatest independence.

If *Professional Education* is often little more than a reworking of its earlier counterpart, it is important for the spirit that pervades it, its attention to male roles and to social and economic issues. Of the English fiction, *Vivian, Patronage,* and *Harrington* are directly influenced by it. And without the arduous preparation for it—so "totally foreign to my habits of thinking or writing,"⁴ Maria confided to Sophy—the Irish novels after *Castle Rackrent* might not have been written at all.

Vivian (1812)

Vivian clearly develops the major themes of *Professional Education,* for the hero's failures in public and private life are directly attributed to character. Charles Vivian has the misfortune to be the only child of a doting, possessive mother whose sole object is her son. And because she "over-educated, over-instructed, over-dosed" him with "premature lessons of prudence," he has not learned to exercise his own judgment or will. Viewed one way, the novel is largely a recital of Vivian's failures, for he is seriously handicapped by irresolution. His unwise choices begin with the decision to postpone marriage to Selina Sidney, the young woman he genuinely loves, until he is of age. After traveling on the continent with his tutor, Russell, he foolishly attempts to emulate the expensive and fashionable tastes of the

Glistonburys by converting his house into a Gothic cathedral. His candidacy in a contested election leads to deeper involvement in a world of political intrigue and to entanglement with fashionable society. By now public opinion aligns him politically with the corrupt Wharton, whose libertine wife entices Vivian to elope with her to the Continent. Since the elopement was planned in scandalous collusion between husband and wife, Vivian is freed of Mrs. Wharton at the same time he loses Selina Sidney as a result of his folly.

His friendship with Lord Glistonbury, an affable but unprincipled peer, involves him more and more in the private lives of Glistonbury's family. Vivian eventually proposes to Glistonbury's vivacious daughter Julia, only to discover that she prefers the tutor Russell. There is yet the daughter Sarah, the "petrified and petrifying" automaton, the last person Vivian would have considered as a wife. The mounting pressures to marry her seem irresistible. Julia believes that Vivian's marriage to Sarah would compensate for his defects in character. Vivian's mother approves the match because of family connection and Lady Sarah's fortune. Now that Glistonbury's son, Lidhurst, has died, the earldom of Glistonbury will devolve to a nephew of Glistonbury unless his daughters marry and have male heirs. If they marry, the title will descend to the first son. Glistonbury's ruling ambition, to change his earldom into a marquisate, means supporting the corrupt political party in power. With Vivian married to Sarah, Glistonbury naturally sees the advantage of his son-in-law's parliamentary support.

Persuaded at last, Vivian says of Sarah, "I like her . . . I really like her" (*TN*, 5:403). The disastrous marriage to Sarah and the political support of Glistonbury mean that Vivian has surrendered his integrity both as private man and public figure. He discovers too late that he has been used as a political pawn by his own father-in-law and is mortified by the partial truth of Wharton's insults. Indeed, Glistonbury has broken his original promise to support Wharton's party; and his desertion of the party and his private negotiations for the marquisate make it appear that Glistonbury has "provided only for himself, his nephew, and his son-in-law" (*TN*, 5:428). In order to preserve some measure of principle and integrity, Vivian challenges Wharton to a duel, which is inevitably fatal to Vivian. The ending suggests that if Vivian has not lived by principle, he dies with honor.

Richard Lovell Edgeworth's *Memoirs* and his preface to *Vivian* both tell us that Maria used the deathbed advice of his mother ("My son, learn early how to say, No!'') as the original idea for the story. Yet when she began to write *Vivian,* she was thinking of another motto as well: "She sees the best & yet the worst pursues," lines written by Thomas Day.[5] Taken together, the mottoes do much to account for a complexity that makes the novel seem much more challenging than a study about irresolution, the purpose according to the preface. The idea that we should resist dangerous temptations is not likely to be missed; yet the story at its best is a subtle probing into human behavior, a study of motives that cause people to manage, repress, and manipulate other people in a world of doubtful values.

The central chapter deals with the education of Glistonbury's daughters, Julia and Sarah. At a more important level, it dramatizes domestic conflict in the private lives of a family, for the real problem begins with the Glistonbury marriage. The starched Lady Glistonbury, long-suffering and dutiful, finds consolation in being a pattern wife and in making her husband miserable. Lord Glistonbury finds temporary solace with a mistress and then channels his private unhappiness into ruthless public ambition. We later see his questionable public life as a reflection of his private unhappiness; his marquisate is a hollow victory, since the dishonorable means used to attain it lead to Vivian's death. The unfortunate marriage means violent disagreements about the education of the daughters so that the two governesses represent the divisive attitudes of father and mother. Glistonbury chooses for the lively Julia an even more spirited and romantically imprudent governess, Miss Bateman. Lady Glistonbury, who thinks of Sarah as an extension of herself, selects the stiff and proper Miss Strictland. As it turns out, the governesses have little influence over their charges. Julia and Sarah are, in fact, helplessly trapped between foolish parents and governesses who function as little more than symbols of parental discord.

Julia's main problem is lack of reserve, yet much of her good sense and maturity is realized through spirited revolt. She defies Miss Bateman by refusing to play the role of Calista in a family theatrical and by being conspicuously absent from a fancy ball that Bateman has arranged. She rejects her mother's old-fashioned notions about submissive duty and chides Vivian for having gone first to her father rather than directly proposing to her: "Men . . . treat woman as puppets, and then wonder that they are not rational creatures!" (*TN,* 5:348). She sees that she was "dogmatically brought up" in ignorance and at one time would have thought it her duty to submit implicitly to parental authority. Yet her judgment has been strengthened through her own reflective experience, and because she is fully in control of head and heart candidly explains to Vivian why she cannot marry him. Later, when her father commands her to accept Vivian's proposal, she chooses banishment over marriage to a man she cannot love. Her impulsiveness, on the other hand, does lead to indiscretion when she unwisely chooses Vivian as confidante and when she proposes to Russell, only to be mortified by the knowledge that he prefers Selina Sidney.

Maria Edgeworth regretted "not having made Selina more interesting"[6] and recognized that she was the type of young woman who would have pleased in real life but not in fiction. On the other hand, she thought Aunt Ruxton would like Julia,[7] an indication of her own approval. The brilliance of Julia's character is dimmed only by the author's failure to take full advantage of her potential, for she has personality as well as character. Sarah, in contrast, is the sister who surprises us most. Before her marriage to Vivian she had been taught that she "should neither read, speak, nor think of love." But now that she is married, her demonstrations of passion are unrepressed, and it becomes her duty to love her husband as much as she can. Love and duty, so pathetically intermingled in Sarah's emotionally deprived life, only alienate Vivian, who is all too familiar with the meaning of restraint.

We see, then, that neither parents nor governesses have any real influence on Julia, yet she is gifted with a remarkable strength of mind and a character that combines both intellect and feeling. Sarah's passion emerges most fully after her marriage to Vivian; yet it is important to see that Sarah's view of marriage as a passport to emotional freedom is significantly influenced by the death of her mother, the one person who had imprisoned her by dutiful restraint. Viewed one way, the tutor Russell does represent, as Hawthorne suggests, the thinking of rational utilitarianism.[8] Yet the author does not make any real point with either his teaching or his pedagogical influence. What matters most is his friendship with Vivian, his well-meant advice that serves largely as a reminder of Vivian's failures. If Julia, Sarah, and Russell seem more important for who they are than for what they represent, it will be worthwhile to look more closely at the hero himself to understand why he "sees the best and yet the worst pursues."

We know from the opening chapter that Vivian lacks judgment, the quality necessary to moral and intellectual independence. His weakness of will stems most obviously from flawed education. Yet what seem more important as the novel progresses are the motives of those who manipulate him to their advantage, the mounting complexity of his entanglements, and his own well-intentioned efforts to make value judgments that make his actions or failures to act seem entirely plausible. Russell's example is less important than the influence of Lady Mary Vivian; indeed, her imposing presence makes her the fullest portrait of a dominating mother in Maria Edgeworth's fiction. Her unwise and often premeditated advice is largely responsible for most of Vivian's indiscretions. In one instance, in particular, when he needs her sympathetic support—in his conviction that Sarah is wrong for him—she virtually forces him to marry a woman he "cannot love, whose person and manners are peculiarly disagreeable" to him.

If Lady Mary manipulates her son for selfish family reasons, Glistonbury governs him for even more impressive public gain. With admirable cunning, he uses the competitive nephew Marmaduke as a means of cementing Vivian's marriage to Sarah. With this point gained, he reasons, the son-in-law will unquestionably support the unpopular political party of the father-in-law. When Glistonbury brings the full force of his powerful personality to bear on the matter, Vivian assumes that his mother will understand his refusal, that she will not encourage a venture that means the loss of her own son's public integrity. But now that Sarah is expecting a child, Lady Mary thinks of the title of marquis that may descend to her grandson. She argues that individuals rarely accomplish much for the public good, reminds Vivian of the expenses of the election, the castle, the coachmaker, the house in town, and entreats her son not to persist in this course of absolute madness. Vivian resists until the last, and rationalize though he may, he cannot justify a compromise in conscience.

Vivian "sees the best and yet the worst pursues," but environment and heredity are made to seem as important as education in shaping his character. Throughout the story, the author views the hero with sympathy. His greatest private indiscretion is his elopement with Mrs. Wharton, yet even at such a moment as this we are told that "he still thought and felt like a man of virtue" (*TN*, 5:310). Because virtue is more nearly a key to his character than vice, it is possible to see James Newcomer's point that the "conclusion is not simply retribution for error but the essential tragedy that derives from the fatal flaw."[9] This does not mean *Vivian* is a great novel or even that it is one of the author's best. What it does suggest is that although the novel is technically imperfect, it still holds our attention, even more by its dramatization of experience than by its exploration of a thesis.

Patronage (1814)

Maria Edgeworth took the idea of *Patronage* from a story her father had invented for family amusement in 1787 when his third wife Elizabeth was recuperating from childbirth. "The Freeman Family," as she called it, was the history of two families, one succeeding by their own merit, the other depending on mean arts and favors of the great. Since the family enjoyed it, she carefully copied it down and twenty-two years later wrote Aunt Ruxton of her plan to use "all that is good in the Freeman Family" as the groundwork for *Patronage*.[10] In August 1809, her father approved the original sketch; yet the writing was often tedious and uninspired and the project became an on-again, off-again affair for the next four years.

It is helpful if we understand both the importance of the undertaking and the difficulties involved in this, the longest and most ambitious of the novels. The story of six young men pursuing five different professions required, to say the least, some knowledge about careers in law and medicine, diplomacy, the church, and military service. Maria Edgeworth realized that the experiences of the young men must be made to seem representative to a reading public prone to compare fictional characters with living people and to criticize misrepresentation or falsity of fact. How might a young soldier or lawyer or physician be expected to think and act? What problems would he face in his career and in society and how would he solve them? And how could the novelist, with limited firsthand exposure to this wide spectrum of experience, provide her usual "truth to life" under such circumstances? It is understandable why she considered the novel a "long pull" and at last grew weary of it. As it turned out, she was obliged to rely heavily on her research for *Professional Education* and on her father's experience and example. There was, in addition, the problem of design, to show why some individuals fail and others succeed in public life. But the greatest problem was the one that plagued her throughout her literary career—how to preserve the interest of the story without sacrificing the moral.

If we examine the moral first, we can easily enough dismiss it as the least important element of the story. The plot of *Patronage,* in keeping with the original design, traces the history of two families, the Falconers and Percys, each family consisting of two parents, three sons, and two daughters. The purpose stated in the preface suggests that the Falconers rise by patronage while the Percys triumph by defying it. Yet Maria Edgeworth's reviewers were among the first to point out that the Percys' success depends heavily on the assistance of others. Mr. Percy is worth listening to, for since he is modeled on the author's father he naturally expresses her own views. Percy's major objection to patronage is that "corrupt, imbecile creatures of patronage" are incapable of directing the affairs of a nation. In his view, patronage means that solicitation and intrigue by incompetents are rewarded over merit earned from honest exertion. In a letter to his son Erasmus, Percy is even more explicit: "partial and pernicious patronage" must be shunned as political favoritism, bestowed without knowledge of merit. On the other hand, assistance based on the recognition of merit should be accepted as just reward (*TN*, 7:230).

The point at issue is not really the principle of patronage at all but the character of those who seek it. Since the Falconer children are victimized by heredity, environment, and education, they would have failed at any undertaking just as surely as the Percys would have succeeded for opposite reasons. The author's preoccupation with the idea of patronage undeniably accounts for most of the novel's technical deficiencies. Yet it is important to see the novel for what it is: a study of behavior at all levels of society, from the drawing room to the court of law, from a waiting maid to a king. Some sixty-five characters weave an elaborate tapestry of the blacks, whites, and greys of human motive, sometimes tedious, sometimes arresting, for the novel often succeeds brilliantly at the level of incident. And for better or worse, it explores more fully than either *Vivian* or *Harrington* the principal themes of *Professional Education*.

The story opens with a shipwreck near the Percy estate. Lost in the wreckage is an important packet of papers belonging to M. de Tourville, an enemy of the powerful political statesman, Lord Oldborough. The packet is found by a Falconer son and partially deciphered by Commissioner Falconer, who discovers in the papers a secret plot to overthrow Oldborough. With three adult sons on his hands, and none of them trained for independent livelihoods, the commissioner seizes opportunity to use the information to family advantage. Hearing that Oldborough will soon visit his estate at Clermont Park and knowing that Mr. Percy is a former friend of the statesman, Falconer begs his cousin Percy for an introduction. For Oldborough, patronage means expediency; "serve me and I will serve you" is a reality of political life. As a result of the packet incident, Falconer's son Cunningham wins a diplomatic assignment by shrewdly disguising his incompetence, but the commissioner is still left with two sons.

John, the least intelligent of the three, succeeds by pure accident: Maria Hauton, Oldborough's sentimental niece, imagines herself in love with him. Since Oldborough needs the niece to further his own political relations with the Duke of Greenwich, he strikes a bargain that seems fair enough to the commissioner: if John is married "elsewhere, within a fortnight," he will be rewarded with a captain's commission and sent abroad, with the promise of rapid advancement within two years. One of the Miss Chattertons might do, the commissioner reflects, but Miss Petcalf "just arrived from India with a large fortune" will do even better. John doltishly objects to Miss Petcalf's dark skin but the problem, father tells son, is "climate—all climate—." Before the fortnight ends, John "looked again and again in the glass to take leave of himself, hung up his flute, and—was married" (*TN,* 7:114). There remains only Buckhurst, the one son who has completed university training. Buckhurst personally prefers the army, but his father urges him to enter the church. As it turns out, Buckhurst, too, is blessed by an accident of fortune: through saving a bishop from suffocation, he is rewarded with a handsome living that would otherwise have been disposed of to one of several worthy clergymen in waiting for it.

At a time when the Falconers seem at the height of prosperity, the Percys are tested by adversity. The dishonest cousin, Robert Percy, with the help of a crooked attorney, takes advantage of a misplaced deed to claim the Percy estate from its rightful owners. The family are forced to take refuge on a small and relatively isolated farm and to accommodate one another in a life of semiretirement. On this situation the author builds a major theme of the plot, since the Percys must demonstrate the triumph of virtue under duress. As the story progresses, the Percy sons succeed through good conduct, diligence, professional competence, and the assistance of friends, while the daughters happily marry the suitors of their choice. In keeping with a proper distribution of poetic justice, Mr. and Mrs. Percy are likewise rewarded for courage and perseverance by being restored to their estate at the end. If the Percys are sometimes tediously exemplary, they do forward a number of ideas important to the Edgeworths'

thinking, and they make those around them all the more interesting
by contrast.

Mr. Percy's role as landlord suggests the advantages of retirement
as a domestic ideal. The greatest advantage is honest independence,
entirely necessary to a man with Percy's temperament and principles.
He admires Oldborough at the same time that he pities him for ov-
erweening ambition and the price he must pay for success in politics:
"a noble mind corroded and debased by ambition—virtuous principle, generous feeling, stifled—a powerful, capacious understanding
distorted" (TN, 7:22). When Percy and his lawyer son Alfred decline
opportunities to serve in Oldborough's cabinet, they say as much
about the dubiousness of politics as about the evils of patronage. But
they also speak directly for the relationship between private and public character and the value Maria Edgeworth places on private happiness. At the end, it is not surprising that Oldborough resigns from
public office or that Count Altenberg, Rosamond Percy's husband,
rejects further service at court. Continuance in either case would have
meant further involvement with the corruptions of power, incompatible with domestic happiness.

The letters that the Percy brothers write home suggest the author's
continuing emphasis on the family. The sons are naturally grateful to
parents who have taught them self-reliance and assisted them in the
choice of careers that will provide independence. Of equal importance
is that their career responsibilities are not incompatible with domestic
pleasure. The serious purpose that underlies the thinking throughout
the novel is that independence is necessary to happiness in public and
private life. In public life, achievement is qualified by the contribution that one is willing to make to society, and reward is the recognition by society of the value of that achievement. The Percy brothers
more often than not express hopes of distinguishing themselves
through their professions. Yet we see that society as a whole is improved through the skills and contributions of young men who are
trained and willing to serve it.

Training, as Alfred makes clear, means something more than spe-
cialization: "the general cultivation of the understanding, and the ac-
quirement of general knowledge, are essential to the attainment of
excellence in any profession" (TN, 7:273). If specialized training does
much to make a competent man, liberal education does more to make
him a good human being. It is not surprising, then, that Alfred admires the chief justice who represents an ideal marriage between pri-

vate man and public figure, between the individual and society. If the relationship between the individual and his larger economic and social context is only one of the concerns of *Patronage,* it does remind us that the author is tackling important public issues. And the real importance of the undertaking, both to her literary career and to the history of the novel, is realized in the Irish novels, where an economic issue often outweighs a romance.

Viewed one way, *Patronage* is a serious study of ideas; viewed in another, parts of it, at least, are an entertaining comedy of manners. The Falconers, quite obviously, are the bad guys who show us in no uncertain terms how to go to the devil. But before admiring them for the wrong reasons, we may as well enlist Maria Edgeworth on our side. Her Aunt Ruxton's dislike of Alfred Percy did not surprise her. As she put the case to her aunt, "He is very stupid & so was every good young man I ever attempted to draw—I am afraid I have no taste for good young men—Buckhurst on the contrary is a universal favorite here with mother daughters & aunts & Fanny literally shed tears for him last night on hearing some of his disasters in the 4th volume".[11] Maria's literary instinct was sound, but the problem might be stated more precisely: in fiction based on formulaic pattern, virtue tends to be abstract, vice concrete. The good people do not have as much to do as the bad, and for this reason the energy and vitality of *Patronage* rely heavily on the Falconers, who provide the story's major conflicts.

The Edgeworth family's liking for Buckhurst Falconer would surely be in keeping with modern preferences. Buckhurst is a multidimensional character who attracts our sympathy for the reason that Rosamond Percy best describes: "There is such a mixture of good and bad in his character, as makes me change my opinion of him every half hour" (*TN,* 7:169). He is scoundrel enough to seduce a young woman, generous enough to defend a friend against a dishonest intrigue by his own brother. Forced by his father into the church, he accepts the calling in a spirit more appropriate to the man than the cloth: "Only make me a dean," he addresses an imagined star of patronage. "Have you not made my brother, the dunce, a colonel? and my brother, the knave, an envoy?—I only pray to be a dean—I ask not yet to be a bishop—you see I have some conscience left" (*TN,* 7:119). As it turns out, he fails in his first appointment, the gift from the bishop, and through his own indiscretion is not offered the living at Chipping-Friars. But the bishop does have a sister—rich,

Mr. Falconer reminds him. "An old, ugly, cross, avaricious devil," Buckhurst replies. There are mounting debts, father reminds son. Buckhurst must marry the bishop's sister, of course, and the note to his family says all that needs to be said: "I was married yesterday, and am as sorry for it to-day as you can be" (*TN*, 7:432).

Oldborough is the most memorable political figure in Maria Edgeworth's fiction. He is prominent throughout most of the novel, a figure of towering strength and personality. His actions are largely a balancing act between friends and enemies so that his greatest challenge becomes the preservation of his own integrity. Admittedly, he sends a Percy son to the fever-infested West Indies and uses a niece as a political pawn; and while such acts are not admirable, they are not unusual in the world of politics (a dubious profession, after all) and not uncommon in a man obsessed with ambition. As a character, he communicates great presence; fortunately, his transition to domestic life comes at the end of the novel, in keeping with the author's preoccupation with private happiness.

If we see the characters in terms of social role, they take on an added dimension of interest by nature of cultural conditioning and the purpose that Maria Edgeworth makes of them. Arabella and Georgiana Falconer are asked to perform parts as fashionable coquettes, and much of the comedy of the Falconer concert, the ball, and the family theatrical derives from the author's exploitation of their attempts to assume a role—from the ineptness of the young women to fit the role to the futile use made of the role to trap men. Lady Angelica Headingham shares the role; she not only exhibits accomplishments but herself becomes an exhibition, a caricature of deluded thinking imposed by the role. In Lady Jane Granville, the role of fashionable lady is, if not exploited, at least explored in a different way. Like Lady Delacour, her attitude toward fashionable society is detached, for she can participate without becoming involved. She shares the conventional belief that a young woman must find a husband, and her main interest is to help Caroline achieve this goal. She is developed sympathetically, with generous heart and motives, and with thinking that is only partially deluded.

Caroline and Rosamond Percy are bound by social roles as well as liberated by them. A young person of sense must be aware of the standards of society considered acceptable. At Mrs. Mortimer's house well-known people from many walks of public life discuss literature and science and issues of public importance—in short, the "best society" as the author interprets it. Caroline and Rosamond are also restricted by the conventions of courtship. In *Vivian,* Julia commits the unpardonable act of proposing to a young man. In *Patronage,* a long discussion between Lady Jane and Caroline centers on whether a woman should show interest in a young man or commit her heart before he makes a declaration. The sisters also have long discussions about love and esteem, with the spirited Rosamond acting as a critic of her sister in a way similarly explored by Lady Delacour in *Belinda.* If Caroline and Rosamond are bound by social limits, they are not trapped by them. Both are given the freedom to choose and in a sense determine their own destinies through their acceptance or rejection of suitors. Maria Edgeworth deprived them of only one freedom, the freedom to make mistakes.

Patronage, like *Vanity Fair,* is a novel without a hero. It is a study of the private and public lives of families, of their relationships among themselves and of their relationships to society at large. It is at once a novel of intrigue, of romance, of problem, of manners. With so many attractive features to reccommend it, it still can hardly be placed among the best fiction. The author herself explained the problem: "I am well aware by woeful experience (vide Patronage) of the danger of making the morality of a fiction too prominent—I have repented—& hope never to be *found out* in a moral again whilst I live."[12] What she may not have realized is how much more she accomplished than the fictional development of a thesis. Nevertheless, since her own reading public lacked enthusiasm for *Patronage,* it might be asking too much to expect the book to improve, like vintage wine, with age. In 1821 a critic for the *Quarterly Review* said for his age what might be equally true for ours: "We should have been more pleased if we had been less taught."[13]

Harrington (1817)

By the time Maria Edgeworth began her literary career, the Jewish villain was a fully constituted stereotype in literature. Edgar Rosenberg describes him as "a fairly thoroughgoing materialist, a physical coward, an opportunist in money matters, a bit of a wizard in peddling his pharmaceautica; queer in his religious observances . . . , clannish in his loyalties, secretive in his living habits, servile in his relations with Christians, whom he abominated; for physical signposts he had an outlandish nose, an unpleasant odor, and frequently

a speech impediment."[14] Since the Tudor Age, the success and pop-
ularity of this stereotype had been ensured by tradition, and during
the early years of the nineteenth century, the Jewish villain continued
to satisfy the reader's demand for the exotic and unusual. In drama
and fiction, he was a societal scapegoat who could be laughed at, imprisoned, shipped off to other continents, or killed in a duel.

Prior to *Harrington,* Maria Edgeworth had done much to embroider
the stereotype, and her earlier stories and novels, as Rosenberg points
out, provide a "fairly thorough cross section of the conventional var-
iants of the Jew-villain".[15] In the children's stories he is a secretive,
underhanded broker ("The Orphans") and a bargaining cheat ("The
Little Merchants"). In the *Moral Tales* he is Solomon, a traitor and
perjurer ("The Prussian Vase") and Mr. Carat, a fraudulent jeweller
("The Good Aunt"). In *Belinda* he is Solomon, the swindler. In *Popular Tales* he is Rachub of El Arish, a money lender who tries to mur-
der his enemies by spreading plague germs in old clothes ("Murad
the Unlucky"). And in *The Absentee* he is Mordicai, a London coachmaker and malicious extortioner. All of these villains are distinguished, in one way or another, by traits common to the Shylock
tradition: dishonesty, usury, cowardice, underhandedness, coarseness,
and vulgarity.

On 7 August 1815, Rachel Mordecai (Lazarus), an American Jewish woman, wrote Maria Edgeworth to complain of the derogatory
manner in which she had depicted Jews. In response, the author
wrote *Harrington* to counteract the "illiberality with which the Jewish
nation had been treated" in some of her works (*TN,* 9:iii). From the
time the book was published, her purpose was criticized. Francis Jeffrey characterized the design as "far too limited for one of her excellent tales."[16] In the late nineteenth century, Helen Zimmern
observed that Maria Edgeworth had to "evolve a Jew out of her moral
consciousness" and that her "elaborate apology is feeble."[17] In this
century, Patrick Murray calls the novel a "qualified act of repentance
for a kind of fictional slander on a people of whom Maria Edgeworth
had no first hand experience."[18] Admittedly, *Harrington* is both awk-
wardly conceived and poorly designed; yet the book is still instructive
for what it attempts to accomplish.

A major concern of the plot is to trace the origin, development,
and disappearance of the hero's prejudice against Jews. In the opening
chapters, the best and most original part of the story, young Harrington, the hero, attempts to investigate his own psyche by recon-

structing his past. In the manner of Pip or David Copperfield, he digs back into his memory of childhood and describes his terrors from a child's point of view: the bobbing silhouette of the lamplighter whose smoking red torch comes nearer and nearer, illuminating "the face and figure of an old man with a long white beard and a dark visage, who, holding a great bag slung over one shoulder, walked slowly on, repeating in a low, abrupt, mysterious tone, the cry of 'Old clothes! Old clothes! Old clothes!' " (*TN*, 9:1). Harrington's nursemaid Fowler sees the extraordinary effect that old Simon the Jew has on the child's imagination and manufactures terrifying stories to frighten him. Since she swears him to keep the stories secret, he becomes victimized in the darkness of night by the terrors of his own imagination: "I saw faces around me grinning, glaring, receding, advancing, all turning at last into the same face of the Jew with the long beard and the terrible eyes; and that bag, in which I fancied were mangled limbs of children—it opened to receive me, or fell upon my bed, and lay heavy on my breast, so that I could neither stir nor scream" (*TN*, 9:4).

Maria Edgeworth's real accomplishment in the opening chapters is that she clearly examines how ideas originate in the consciousness through association. In *Practical Education* she had defined taste as a formation of ideas grounded firmly on knowledge and experience. Furthermore, taste can only be developed through education and must begin with carefully selected objects of association. Harrington's childhood attitudes toward Jews are negative, shaped as they are by the stories of a vicious nursemaid, by education (books that portray Jews unfavorably), and by the views of prejudiced parents (Mr. Harrington votes against the Naturalization Bill). The elder Harringtons further encourage their son's bias by violating child-rearing practices that the Edgeworths stressed in *Practical* and *Professional Education*. Mr. Harrington encourages his young son to prattle unflattering opinions about Jews before adult company (a child should never be used as an exhibition) and rewards him with cake and wine for his absurd little exhibitions of wit (an improper association of a reward with behavior). Mrs. Harrington interprets her son's vivacity as genius (the Edgeworths virtually denied the existence of innate genius) and boasts of her son's lively imagination to her fashionable friends.

Such practices should not bode well for Harrington; and to make matters worse, he is sent to a public school (a practice discouraged in both *Practical* and *Professional Education*). Here he meets Mowbray, a school bully and the leader of a party of anti-Jewish sympathizers, who mercilessly persecute a Jewish peddler named Jacob. Presumably, this incident is a major step in Harrington's learning process, since he begins to sympathize with the Jew's humility and suffering. But then Maria Edgeworth converts him, as Elizabeth Eisenstadt points out, "with improbable rapidity from an enemy to a friend of the Jews."[19] At the end of his public school training (and before he goes to Cambridge), he confesses that he has "long since got rid of the foolish prejudices of my childhood" (*TN*, 9:29). The problem is that after showing in detail how Harrington acquired his anti-Semitic prejudices, Maria Edgeworth does not convincingly represent him conquering them. What to do with him after his conversion is a major technical problem during the remainder of the story, and the author is forced to rely heavily on contrivance to sustain the story and resolve the complications of the plot.

During his three years at Cambridge, Harrington meets Israel Lyons, a distinguished Jewish author and scholar. Lyons is not dramatically developed as a character, but Maria Edgeworth includes him for several reasons: to advance the hero's learning process (his character is strengthened through association with good companions); to break down the Jewish stereotype (Lyons is a man of genius); and to provide the hero, through Lyons's letter, with an introduction to Mr. Montenero and his daughter, Berenice, Sephardic Jews now visiting England from America. Lyons, however, is little more than a stereotype of the "Saintly Jew,"[20] and the reader's view of him is unfortunately restricted by the author's limited treatment of him.

Interestingly enough, these are not problems in the development of Mr. Montenero who, according to Rosenberg, "represents the first full-length portrayal of a sympathetic Jew in the whole of the English novel".[21] A banker and philanthropist, Montenero is fully convincing as a patient, wise man who eventually rescues Harrington's father from the threat of bankruptcy. With the introduction of the Monteneros, the plot promises to be a conventional love story (hero meets, woos, and wins heroine), since Harrington falls in love with the beautiful Berenice. But social realities create narrative problems for the author: Berenice is Jewish and Harrington is Gentile. Harrington, of course, has long ago conquered his anti-Semitic prejudices, and a difference in religion is not significant to him. Nevertheless, the possibility of his marrying a Jewish woman arouses alarming objections from his Gentile family and friends who are all traditionally prejudiced against Jews.

Maria Edgeworth, like George Eliot after her, treats the problem of anti-Semitism sociologically by deploying a number of its causes over a full spectrum of society. The elder Mr. Harrington's anti-Semitism is politically based in a world of men who think of Jews as guileful adventurers. Mrs. Harrington and her friends, Lady de Brantefield and Mrs. Coates, represent the world of fashion, and their attitudes toward Jews are distinguished by varying circumstances. Mrs. Harrington suffers from a nervous disposition, and her dreams and omens only confirm her susceptibility to suspicion; for her, the Jew, by his very nature, is a source of mischief. Lady de Brantefield's prejudices are rooted in a family tradition in which ancestors tortured and executed Jews for horrible crimes. She sees Jews as cheats and swindlers "from the very dregs of the people." Mrs. Coates, a product of ignorance and superstition, believes that certain diseases may be fatal "where there was any Jewish taint in the blood" and that "a Jewish heart might be harder to break than another's." In her judgment, Jews are unsocial, revengeful, and suspicious people. Mowbray represents the type of anti-Jewish feeling likely to be found among military officers: during his military experience at Gibralter, he taunts Jacob (who has come there for employment) as a "young Shylock" and "Wandering Jew."

Harrington's desire to marry Berenice is thwarted not only by societal bias, but by another obstacle even more threatening. Mowbray, anti-Semite though he is, decides to compete with Harrington for Berenice's hand and attempts to impress her through guile and flattery. In truth, he is interested solely in her fortune, but in his proposal to her he offers to "sacrifice religion—everything to love. He was refused irrevocably" (*TN*, 9:134). Recognizing that he has lost Berenice to his rival, Mowbray attempts to slander Harrington by enlisting old Fowler to testify that her former charge suffers from insanity. The hero's predicament—his parents' threat to disinherit him if he marries a Jewish woman and Mr. Montenero's view of insanity as an "invincible obstacle" to marriage—now becomes the major conflict in the plot.

Mr. Montenero's acceptance of Harrington as a son-in-law is governed by two conditions: the young man must demonstrate that he can discipline his enthusiastic temperament, and the charge of insan-

ity must be removed. To meet the first condition, he is tested by
experiences designed to arouse his enthusiasm and fear. During a visit
with Mowbray and the Monteneros to the Tower of London, Harrington kneels to pay homage to the empty armor of the Black Prince,
rants Clarence's dream from Shakespeare, and soliloquizes from Ak-
enside's "Pleasures of the Imagination." Later, during a visit to the
Jewish synagogue, he is emotionally unsettled by a Jewish appara-
tion, "a figure exactly resembling one of the most horrible of the Jewish figures which used to haunt me when I was a child." As Jeffrey
points out, such incidents do little more than characterize the hero as
a "very silly and contemptible blockhead."[22] What Maria Edgeworth
wants us to see is, of course, clear: that Harrington's childhood attitudes toward Jews were based on associations of fear and terror, and
that first impressions which are made on the imagination are "seldom
entirely effaced from the mind" (PE, 216).

Nevertheless, we discover that Harrington's behavior has been encouraged all along by Mowbray's tediously contrived scheme to prove
the hero insane. The figure, dressed up to so little purpose in the
synagogue, is none other than Fowler, who is later forced to confess
her intrigues as an accomplice in Mowbray's plans. Mowbray is killed
in a duel with a fellow officer, and Fowler, following her confession,
is to be shipped off to America. Thus, the second condition is now
met. Mr. Montenero is convinced that young Harrington is a man of
principle and honor and in saving the hero's father from bankruptcy,
wins his respect and gratitude.

It would seem, then, that all obstacles are cleared for the wedding:
the hero has long ago given up his prejudices, he has learned self-
control, and his presumed insanity has been proven false. Old Mr.
Harrington has been humbled and awed by Montenero's financial
generosity toward him: "Can you conceive, Mr. Montenero . . . that
after all I have seen of you—all you have done for me—can you conceive me to be such an obstinately prejudiced brute? My prejudices
against the Jews I give up—you have conquered them—all, all" (TN,
9:203). Then follows Mr. Montenero's dramatic disclosure: "I have
tried you to the utmost, and am satisfied both of the steadiness of
your principles and of the strength of your attachment to my daughter—Berenice is not a Jewess" (TN, 9:203). She is, Montenero continues, "A Christian—a Protestant . . . an English Protestant . . .
Daughter of an English gentleman of good family" (TN, 9:203). The
ending merits Frank Modder's judgment that "the whole fabric which

the novelist has raised falls suddenly before the single fact that Berenice is the child of a Christian mother, and that she was christened in her infancy."[23] Having adopted a conventional plot as a means of making the story attractive, Maria Edgeworth has problems in resolving it conventionally since she has chosen a Jewish heroine and a Gentile hero.[24]

In spite of the feeble ending, *Harrington* is important for what it attempted and for the historical importance that this gives it. The opening chapters, as we have seen, examine the validity of consciousness as a means of perception; and in this sense the book provides an interesting exploration of a dimension of human psychology. Yet prejudice is shown to be both a psychological and social phenomenon, at once the outgrowth of faulty associations in childhood and the product of social conditioning. The book attempts to explore social influences that make people what they are. Ignorance, fear, and superstition characterize all levels of society, regardless of class, and the Gentile characters provide a variety of opinions on the Jewish issue, a panoramic view of intolerance that leads to injustice in society as a whole. To avoid forming "uncharitable judgments either of individuals or nations" one must be "well-educated and well informed." In this sense, *Harrington* develops one of the principal themes of *Professional Education*—the necessity of moral independence—since the hero's experience and observations enable him to acquire a character that is stable and respected.

Maria Edgeworth was not satisfied with *Harrington*. In retrospect, she thought the novel "should have been a strong picture of a great character resisting persecution"[25]—a story altogether different from the one she wrote. The ending, she said, "was an Irish blunder, which, with the best intentions, I could not avoid".[26] The best of intentions cannot produce a good novel in *Harrington*. Yet it still merits attention as a pioneering attempt to explore the origins of a character's psyche and as a milestone in the portrayal of civilized Jewish types. As Modder remarks, "*Harrington* is significant as the first work to advertise the fact that a Jew may be a gentleman merchant, like Mr. Montenero; a gentleman professor of Hebrew like Israel Lyons; a gentleman old-clothes-man, like Simon the Jew; and an honest peddler, like Jacob the Jew . . . . The novel thus deserves notice because it marks a departure in the interpretation of Jews in the everyday life of modern England".[27]

Chapter Five
The Education of a Nation

Castle Rackrent, Ennui, The Absentee, and *Ormond* were all written for the edification of an English audience. At the end of *Rackrent* the editor (speaking for the author) remarked that "the domestic habits of no nation in Europe were less known to the English than those of their sister country, till within these few years."[1] And only two years before her death, Maria Edgeworth alluded to Archbishop Whately's remark that "it is impossible to conceive how ignorant the English still are of Ireland, and how positive in their ignorance."[2] The two statements are separated by forty-seven turbulent years of Irish history, and for thirty of those years the author of *Castle Rackrent* viewed her country in silence: "The people would only break the glass, and curse the fool who held the mirror up to nature—distorted nature, in a fever."[3] What matters, of course, is that *Rackrent* began the course of Irish fiction and that other Irish novelists followed Maria Edgeworth's lead in attempting to represent Ireland "as it really is."

The Irish novel in the early decades of the nineteenth century was, in Thomas Flanagan's words, "a kind of advocacy before the bar of English public opinion."[4] This is not surprising when we remember that the English reader knew almost nothing about Ireland. News about some hideous insurrection or agrarian outrage might remind him of the country's existence; but as Maria Edgeworth points out, he was virtually ignorant about the Irish people and the nature of Irish society. There was both a desire and a need for accurate information about Ireland, and the novel was considered a proper vehicle for providing such information. The Ireland of Maria Edgeworth's generation was a country fiercely divided by issues of race, religion, and nationality. To represent the country "as it really is"—or as it then appeared—was no simple task for the novelist. Catholic emancipation, the condition of the peasantry, and questions of land ownership and absenteeism—problems rooted deeply in the history of Ireland's tragic past—were themes that understandably engaged the novelist's imagination. In her four novels of Irish life, her special task was to represent Ireland as accurately as she could and explain and

94

interpret what was characteristic and original about Irish society. Her Irish novels thus have special value, in addition to their artistic merit, as the unique record of a culture.

Castle Rackrent (1800)

Sometime between 1793 and 1795 Maria Edgeworth amused her Aunt Ruxton by mimicking the gestures and manner of John Langan, the old family steward. She agreed with her aunt's suggestion that the old man might be an appealing prototype for a fictional character and began to write, as fast as her pen would go, the history of a family as told by an old Irish retainer, Thady Quirk. Sir Condy's story, the last and longest of the four segments that make up the story, was added two years later, and the little book bearing the title *Castle Rackrent* was published anonymously in January 1800. The success of this first novel was so great that in the year of its first appearance some unknown person attempted to claim authorship. After reading it, George III is reported to have "rubbed his hands & said what what—I know something now of my Irish subjects."[5] Pitt likewise admired it, and Lord Carhampton, the Irish commander in chief in 1796–97, called it the "best book he [had] read since he learnt to read."[6] By 1810 the book was ready for a fifth edition, and Maria Edgeworth's reputation as a novelist was assured.

Castle Rackrent, according to the original title page, is "Taken From Facts, And From The Manners of the Irish Squires, Before the Year 1782." The subtitle and its date are important to the author's intention; as we shall see, the book was written with a decisive purpose, and her fear that the purpose would be misunderstood was one reason for her own disapproval of the novel.[7] The plot is largely Thady's account of the decline and fall of four successive generations of Rackrent squires. Sir Patrick, the first of the landlords, is a hard-drinking, festive, and jovial country gentleman who gives the "finest entertainment ever was heard of in the country" and fits out the chicken house for the nightly overflow of guests. Drinking ironically distinguishes his life and causes his death: "just as the company rose to drink his health with three cheers, he fell down in a sort of fit, and was carried off" (*CR,* 11). People from far and near flock to the funeral to get a glimpse of the hearse. As the procession moves through Patrick's own town, the body is seized for debt, with angry curses from the mob as the last forlorn tribute to his memory.

The generous Sir Patrick is succeeded by Sir Murtagh, an avaricious skinflint who uses the law to exact fines and penalties from the poor tenantry. "Every thing upon the face of the earth furnished him good matter for a suit," says Thady: "His herriots and duty work brought him in something—his turf was cut—his potatoes set and dug—his hay brought home, and in short all the work about his house done for nothing; for in our leases there were strict clauses with heavy penalties, which Sir Murtagh knew well how to enforce" (*CR,* 14–15). Lady Murtagh takes advantage of the tenants' fear of lawsuits to get cheap labor and to fleece them of household staples: "Her table . . . kept for next to nothing—duty fowls, and duty turkies, and duty geese, came as fast as we could eat 'em, for my lady kept a sharp look out, and knew to a tub of butter every thing the tenants had, all round" (*CR,* 14). Murtagh digs up a fairy mound, against Thady's advice, and luck turns against him. If Heaven had spared him, Thady tells us, he would surely have won the suit against the Nugents, "a plump two thousand a year." He catches cold in attending court and breaks a blood vessel while quarreling with his wife about the renewal of a lease: "All the law in the land could do nothing in that case" (*CR,* 18).

Sir Kit, Sir Murtagh's improvident successor, "valued a guinea as little as any man—money to him was no more than dirt" (*CR,* 20). A young rake and fortune hunter, he is interested in the estate only as a means of supporting his lavish tastes for gallantry and gaming in Bath. As Thady tells it, he "left all to the agent, and though he had the spirit of a Prince, and lived away to the honour of his country abroad, which I was proud to hear of, what were we the better for that at home?" (*CR,* 20). Kit's constant demands for money are satisfied by the agent's grinding the face of the poor: "Rents must be all paid up to the day, and afore—no allowance for improving tenants—no consideration for those who had built upon their farms" (*CR,* 21). Old tenants are turned out, land is advertised to the highest bidder, and farms are finally rented below value to provide the master with ready cash. When money can no longer be supplied from bond or mortgage or tenants, the agent is turned out and Thady's son Jason, "who had corresponded privately with his honor occasionally on business," is appointed to the post.

Interestingly enough, this does not improve Sir Kit's fortunes, and in a desperate gamble in the matrimonial lottery he marries the "grandest heiress in England" to recoup his fortunes. The "pretty Jessica" of courtship days becomes a "stiff-necked Israelite" who cannot be parted from her jewels after marriage. Kit locks her away in her room for seven years while he entertains lavishly and contributes to the spiraling debts against an estate now heavily mortgaged to Jason. Kit is eventually killed in a duel, and his lady "returned thanks for this unexpected interposition in her favour, when she had least reason to expect it." (*CR*, 34). Jessica returns to England, and Sir Condy, the last of the landlords and Thady's favorite, arrives to complete what his predecessors had so well begun: the dissolution of a family lineage and the destruction of an estate that had flowered with early hopes of prosperity.

Condy, like Patrick, represents a "monument of old Irish hospitality," and it seems appropriate that the last of the Rackrents should reverence the memory of the first by erecting a handsome gravestone in his honor. Because of Thady's indulgence and partiality as a narrator, he tends to emphasize Condy's warm heart and generous nature and blunt the fact that he is no more able than his predecessors to manage his life and property. A tossed-up coin determines Condy's choice of a wife, but the Banshee is now very close to his window. Isabella's family withhold her dowry because she marries Condy, but the two set out with reckless abandon to perpetuate the myth of Sir Patrick's grandeur. Guests guzzle whiskey punch in the growing dusk of a drawing room, for there are no candles in the house, no horse to go for any "but one that wanted a shoe," no "turf in for the parlour and above stairs, and scarce enough for the cook in the kitchen" (*CR*, 53).

As the creditors close in, Jason provides Condy with cash by buying the lodge "for little or nothing" (*CR*, 54). Condy spends lavishly on his election to the Irish Parliament, where he votes "against his conscience very honorably" for the Patriot party and loses his chance of office. Isabella knows that Condy is ruined and leaves him on the eve of disaster with "an execution against the goods coming down, and the furniture to be canted, and an auction in the house all next week" (*CR*, 68). Only Condy and Thady are left in the castle, and Condy attempts to stave off the reality of loans and bills with whiskey punch. Jason manipulates him skillfully in acquiring Isabella's jointure. For three hundred golden guineas Condy signs away the final shred of his claim to the estate, and symbolically drinks a toast from Sir Patrick's great horn. A few hours later Condy is dead and Thady, still "following the fortunes of them that have none left," tells us that Condy's funeral was but a poor spectacle after all.

Castle Rackrent is not Maria Edgeworth's only fine novel, but it is her most celebrated one because of a uniformly successful blending of form, style, and characterization. In this century the novel has been interpreted as a chronicle of the eighteenth-century Irish squirearchy and of the corrupt social, economic, and political conditions that made the gentry irresponsible and the peasantry miserable.[8] Thady has been viewed both as a villain who assists Jason in bringing about the downfall of the Rackrent family[9] and, more subtly, as the ironic exemplar of "passive participation in evil."[10] Scott admired the "immortal Thady" who could see that his masters were not always right but could not puzzle out why they were wrong.[11] Critics in this century, following Scott's lead, have almost uniformly judged Thady as "unreliable," and since this is so the story is "as final and as damning a judgment as English fiction has ever passed on the abuse of power and the failure of responsibility."[12]

There is the question, too, of Maria Edgeworth's superior attitude toward the lower Irish. Of *Castle Rackrent,* Altieri points out Maria's weaknesses in italicizing "catachreses, phonetic spellings, and Irish idioms" to assure the reader that she does not share the grammatical idiosyncrasies of her characters.[13] And Brookes adds that "the wit involved in Thady's witless narration makes the reader feel superior to its perpetrator, makes him share with the author the sense of superiority of a mind ordered sufficiently to see the mistake that is being made."[14] The book certainly invites us to make all of these judgments, but it does not require that we make them. And it may be helpful to piece together the background of this original story in an attempt to see what Maria Edgeworth herself had in mind.

Castle Rackrent is cast in the form of a memoir with the author posing as editor and Thady serving as observer-narrator. The preface makes an important distinction between the biographer who can form ethical judgments about the private lives of individuals and the historian who "can seldom . . . pause to illustrate this truth" (*CR,* 2). Since the biographer's privileged position may encourage him to abuse his talents, it is better that Thady tell his own "plain unvarnished tale" as the most likely means of establishing truth. In the preface Maria Edgeworth refers to Thady as "honest" and in her own person as editor at the end she describes him as "faithful." The purpose of the book is to lay "before the English reader . . . a specimen of manners and characters, which are perhaps unknown in England" (*CR,* 97).

The truth that Maria Edgeworth claims for the book is less a truth to fiction than a truth to life, verifiable by fact.[15] And her carefully worded "specimen of manners and characters" means that she wanted to share with the English reader the mixture of "quickness, simplicity, cunning, carelessness, dissipation, disinterestedness, shrewdness and blunder" (*CR*, 97), characteristic of a people that she now claimed as her own. If she relinquished history for biography (or more accurately, autobiography), she also laid aside morals for manners, a chance she was unwilling to hazard in the later Irish novels. The world of *Castle Rackrent* is neither moral nor immoral, but amoral; and the characters who inhabit it are selected as representatives of certain types of manners and behavior.

One way in which this truth to fact is reflected is in Thady Quirk's language and syntax, a fairly accurate transcription of the Irish peasant speech that Maria Edgeworth knew. Her interest in speech patterns is shown in the *Essay on Irish Bulls* (1802), an able defense of the language spoken by the lower classes in Ireland, as well as a criticism of English prejudice and ignorance. According to the *Essay,* a "bull" is a speech and/or behavioral blunder, and if not less common to Ireland than to other countries, it provides much of the characteristic expressiveness and color of Irish language and culture. It means not only "quickness of repartee, but cleverness in action . . . with no slight mixture of cunning"; it employs a "superfluity of wit and metaphor," a "sort of cool good sense and dry humour," mixed with "keen satire." Eleven species of tropes and figures that, in one way or another, alter meaning are listed in the "Bath Coach Conversation" in the *Essay.* It is the persistent use of these and other figures, often recurring in rapid succession, that gives the density and flavor of real life to the pages of *Rackrent*.

One of the most frequently recurring figures is anticlimax. For example, Thady says of Sir Patrick, "Poor gentleman! he lost a fine hunter and his life, at last . . . all in one day's hunt" (*CR*, 9). Or of Sir Kit, Thady remarks, "He looked to me no more like himself than nothing at all" (*CR*, 25). When Sir Kit's wife is disappointed by the few bonfires that welcome her to Castle Rackrent, Thady explains the problem to her in this way: "My lady . . . there would have been fifty times as many, but for fear of the horses and frightening your ladyship" (*CR*, 25). In another instance, when Sir Kit's wife becomes ill, Thady observes, "My lady had a sort of fit, and it was given out she was dead, by mistake" (*CR*, 32). Finally, Sir Condy erects a gravestone in Sir Patrick's honor, "setting forth in large letters his age, birth, parentage, and many other virtues" (*CR*, 37). Since drinking not only dominated Patrick's life but also caused his death, the "virtues" on his tombstone are ironically restricted to the chronological facts of his life.

A number of Thady's remarks are examples both of hyperbole and antanaclasis (double meaning). We see, for instance, that Sir Murtagh does not consider sturdy fencing a benefit to the estate: "There was always some tenant's pig, or horse, or cow, or calf, or goose, trespassing, which was so great a *gain* to Sir Murtagh that he did not like to hear me talk of repairing fences" (*CR*, 14; my italics). In another instance, we are told that Sir Kit's creditors haunt "him up and down, day and night, who had nothing to lose" (*CR*, 23). Sir Kit literally has nothing to lose since he has squandered his money at the gambling table, and his creditors would likewise have nothing to gain by finding him. In addition to anticlimax, hyperbole, and antanaclasis, Thady's idiom is distinguished by other colloquial and individualizing figures: by metaphor ("The bride might well be a great fortune"); by rhetorical modification ("Out of forty-nine suits which he had, he never lost one but seventeen"); by epizeuxis ("indeed, indeed," "often and often," "at all, at all"); and by hysteron proteron (a humorous interchange of words—"The short and the long of it was . . . ").

In her introduction to the *Essay on Irish Bulls*, Maria Edgeworth observes that the bull "branches into innumerable ramifications," and for this reason the characteristics of the idiom cannot always be neatly labeled; they can only be described. Near the beginning, Thady says of the dead Sir Patrick, "Long life to him!" And near the end, Judy M'Quirk, Thady's great niece, has missed Sir Condy's mock wake because she has been away attending a wedding: " 'but (says she) it won't be so, I hope, the next time, please your honor.' " Thady's speech, as Altieri suggests, "is a picture of the novel's world."[16]

But like many modern critics, Altieri perceives the language of *Rackrent* as a vehicle for the author's negative judgments about that world. And while the novel may support such an interpretation, it is safe to say that it is not representative of Maria Edgeworth's personal views, which are persuasively outlined in her review of John Carr's *The Stranger in Ireland* (1807). Taxing Carr with factual errors, a "trivial and inflated" style, and indiscriminate praise, the author turns in the latter part of the essay to her own enlightened views of the causes of Ireland's misery and of solutions most likely to bring about positive change: "All signs of party hatred should be suppressed; all party words forborn. The appellations of orangeman and *croppies* should never be heard: *Protestant ascendancy* should never be talked of; nor should the term *an honest man* be used exclusively to designate a Protestant."[17] Significantly, however, she compliments Carr for his "faithful representation" of the Irish peasantry and offers a generous extract with the hope that it will strengthen public interest in their favor.

Maria Edgeworth's generous sympathy and compassion for the Irish peasantry are also revealed in her detailed and illuminating notes appended to Mrs. Leadbeater's *Cottage Dialogues* (1811). These notes, in fact, help clarify the inconsistencies and contradictions in the author's peasant characters that have puzzled modern critics. For example, Watson remarks, "We are shown good reason why Thady should love his masters, none at all why he should respect them as he does."[18] Yet the notes point out that "there cannot be more generous spirits, more grateful dispositions to work upon, than those of the Irish, when they are kindly treated."[19] Thady's loyalty to the family is the honor of a peasant's code of values, and his opinions of the landlords depend on their treatment of him. Thady prefers Condy over the other landlords because of Condy's generous nature (as opposed to the skinflint nature of Murtagh or of Sir Kit's middleman) and because Condy does not act "high" toward him.

On the other hand, Thady dislikes his son Jason who, after purchasing Condy's lodge, becomes "quite a great gentleman" and looks down on Thady. Thady's expression, "Long may he live to reign over us," we find from the author's notes, is a form of benediction of the lower Irish;[20] and Thady's belief that if Sir Kit returned "he'd see us righted" typifies the peasant's mixed trust in Providence.[21] The world of *Castle Rackrent* makes better sense if we know that the peasant's ruling passions are the "love of power, of money, of friends, or of long life."[22] And if we add to these passions his trust in luck[23] and his reliance on "favour and affection,"[24] his character and the story that he tells seem more comprehensible.

Despite the novel's manifest appeal to readers for almost two centuries, O'Connor observes that "we do not care for any of its characters because none of them belongs to civilized society, and the novel presupposes a civilized society."[25] It does not, of course, any more than *Wuthering Heights*, presuppose such a society. It presupposes only

a world as viewed by an illiterate old peasant whose foibles, prejudices, and idiosyncrasies cause us to love him better and remember
him longer than almost any other character in Maria Edgeworth's fiction. The world that he creates for us emerges from strange and foreign paradoxes so that we are jolted into fitting together the pieces—
love or money, money or love, luck and duty, cash and land. If trouble is business, business is also trouble, and the landlords that Thady
describes make a muddle of things when business and trouble are
combined.

Thady's peasant voice levels all distinctions so that the characters
are ethically equalized. The tenantry are no happier to see Lady Murtagh depart than she is to be gone. Sir Kit's death means Jessica's
double freedom from husband and from locked-up imprisonment, and
Kit's "loss to society" is judged inconsolable only by those who will
no longer profit from winning gambling debts from him. The ladies
who visit Jessica are prompted less by paying respect than by malicious curiosity about her diamonds. Isabella marries Condy, not for
love, but to spite her family. And Condy's friends help him win an
election only that they may collect from him for their pains and
thereby contribute to his financial ruin.

Jason is generally viewed as the villain of the piece, but he is finally no better or worse than anybody else. Before the lodge transac-
tion, Jason "explained matters out of the face to Sir Conolly, and
made him sensible of his embarrassed situation" (CR, 41). Seeing
that Condy is "not willing to take his affairs into his own hands, or
to look them even in the face" (CR, 41), Jason then becomes an opportunist. When Thady pleads with him to show Condy mercy, Jason's candid response comes as close to a value judgment as anything
in the novel: "Who will he find to use him better?" (CR, 77). The
book's ending invites us to share Flanagan's belief that "Jason's character shows a shrewd understanding on Maria's part of the new class
which was rising to power."[26] Yet Thady's conclusion is as ambiva-
lent as the narrator's story itself. "Others say, Jason won't have the
lands at any rate—many wishes it so" (CR, 96). And as to the Union,
approved six months after Castle Rackrent was published, the editor
cannot predict whether it will "hasten or retard the amelioration of
this country" (CR, 97). Perhaps the best that can be hoped is the
introduction of British manufacturers as replacements for the men of
education who will leave Ireland for England. Maria Edgeworth lived
long enough to know that British manufacturers were not the solu-

tion to Ireland's problems. And twenty-seven years after *Rackrent* was published, she doubted that "manufactures" had contributed either to the moral or intellectual improvement of the people of England.[27]

Castle Rackrent is remarkable not only for the contrast it presents to Maria Edgeworth's other works but for being, in Flanagan's words, "that rare event, an almost perfect work of fiction."[28] The perfection stems from the harmony of images and impressions, from the vigor and color of symbol and tone. Old Thady is chipped and chiseled from the reality of a peasant world that Maria Edgeworth knew well. The story that he tells is a piecing together of fact and fiction, dominated always by his whimsical attitudes, as unsettling as they are ambiguous. The novel succeeds brilliantly because it for once fully accomplished the author's purpose: the presentation of a "specimen of manners and characters."[29] If we view it this way, we are not required to use labels or to make judgments about the moral and mental confusion of the lower Irish or to see the author or ourselves as consciously superior to the Irish peasantry. Her lessons for the English and Irish were the same, but her attitudes, if they differ at all, are more sympathetic toward her adopted countrymen.[30]

When Richard Lovell Edgeworth arrived home and scribbled off a few lines for a preface to *Castle Rackrent,* neither he nor his daughter could know that it would begin the course of regional fiction, that it was the first novel to treat the Irish peasantry seriously, the first to be written in the Irish vernacular.[31] Nor could they foresee its influence on Scott and his disciples.[32] Nevertheless, Maria Edgeworth was afraid that she had offended the Irish and set out, in her next novel of Irish life, to make amends.

Ennui (1809)

Ennui was first written in 1804 and then entirely rewritten before publication. The title is indicative of the foreboding purpose stated in the preface: "The causes, curses, and cure of this disease are exemplified . . . in such a manner, as not to make the remedy worse than the disease" (*TN,* 4:211). The plots of *Ennui, The Absentee,* and *Ormond* are all formed from a recipe that combines education, romance, and Irish life, but the ingredients are blended least skillfully in *Ennui.* Lord Glenthorn, the hero, is Irish born, but the major portion of his rather useless life has been spent in fashionable dissipation in London. The early chapters paint a tedious picture of the hero's epicurism, his precipitant marriage and divorce, his dominance by a household of unruly servants and parasitical companions, and his thoughts of suicide—problems stemming largely from a condition described as ennui. At a more important level, the hero's shallowness is the result of erratic and undisciplined education, a problem he is unequipped to handle.

As early as "Angelina" and "Forester" Maria Edgeworth showed that she could develop an educational theme with intelligent sensitivity, yet the cure for boredom and laziness is not here satisfactorily resolved. Glenthorn's discovery that he is the son of the old Irish nurse Ellinor and not the real earl of Glenthorn; his generous but improbable surrender of wealth, title, and estate to Christy O'Donohue, the rightful earl, reared as the peasant son of Ellinor; and his study of law, his rapid professional rise, and his marriage to Cecilia Delamere, heir-at-law to the Glenthorn estate, are sufficient testimony to the novel's weaknesses of plotting without need for further rehearsal.

What is more significant is that in the central chapters the rather colorless hero becomes secondary to the larger interest in Irish society so that his ignorance is turned to advantage. On his arrival in Dublin, he is as surprised, as the Edgeworths themselves must have been in 1782, at "instances of grand beginnings and lamentable want of finish, with mixture of the magnificient and the paltry" (TN, 4:242). As he journeys farther toward his own estate, he experiences his first shocking confrontation with the country's poor, squalid, and illiterate peasantry: "From the inn yard came a hackney chaise, in a most deplorable crazy state . . . one door swinging open, three blinds up, because they could not be let down . . . The horses were worthy of the harness; wretched little dog-tired creatures . . . their bones starting through their skin; one lame, the other blind; one with a raw back, the other with a galled breast" (TN, 243).

On the fourth day he is nearing his own castle in one of the wildest and most secluded parts of Ireland; then follows a brief but romantically haunting scene when Glenthorn sees his own territories by moonlight—the stunted trees bent by ocean winds, the huge shadows of rocks on the water, the silence broken by carriage wheels rolling over the sand. The castle suddenly appears in full gloomy grandeur with pointed arches and turrets and battlements; hollow sounds of horses' feet are heard as the carriage crosses over a drawbridge, and the strange, eager voices of a ragged multitude greet the newly arrived lord. It is as meaningful a signal as anything in Maria Edgeworth's fiction of the arrival of a stranger in a strange land.

Once home on his estate, Glenthorn is initiated into two phases of Irish experience: the life of the landlord, with its attendant public character and responsibilities, and the social life among the gentry. Since Glenthorn insists on taking estate matters into his own hands, he is forced to realize his appalling ignorance of an alien culture divided by issues of land, education, and religion. Mr. M'Leod, his Scottish agent, is, of course, modeled after Maria's father, and his management of the Glenthorn estate is a close transcript of Richard Lovell Edgeworth's own practice as landlord in 1782. This may partially explain M'Leod's success as a character: the slow-paced cadences of his speech, his hesitant manner, his deliberate reasoning are the mark of a man whose wisdom has been earned from experience. On the other side of the coin is the selfish and opinionated Mr. Hardcastle, agent for the neighboring Ormsby estate, who is everything that M'Leod is not. In Hardcastle's opinion, the tenants are no better than serfs: "Keep the Irish common people ignorant, and you keep 'em quiet; and that's the only way with them; for they are too quick and smart, as it is, naturally" (*TN*, 4:267–68). If M'Leod and Hardcastle represent two opposing views of resident landlord management, Glenthorn serves as a kind of balance that makes the contrast meaningful.

As an alien, he cannot fully grasp the lessons that M'Leod attempts to teach him—that the neatness, order, economy, and activity that he sees among the tenantry are the product of twenty-six years of patient work. M'Leod's school, attended by both Catholics and Protestants, is a small-scale demonstration of how religious differences might be solved, how associations and habits might be changed over a period of time. All of this means little to Glenthorn at the time since, as a fashionable upper-class Englishman, he has been led to believe that money has the magic of Aladdin's lamp. The failure of his scheme to befriend old Ellinor (his real mother) with a neat English-style cottage is symptomatic of the larger social and economic barriers between two national cultures. And since Glenthorn is free to make his own mistakes, his rash generosity and mistaken benevolence round out a brief but careful study of landlord behavior and estate management. The conclusion that he reaches is as timely for a nation as for an individual: "In the impatience of my zeal for improvement,

I expected to do the work of two hundred years in a few months: and because I could not accelerate the progress of refinement in this miraculous manner, I was out of humour with myself and with a whole nation" (*TN,* 4:276).

The fashionable parties at Ormsby Villa introduce Glenthorn to social life among the Irish gentry, and Maria Edgeworth's humorous, satirical delineations of manners and morals suggests that the Irish upper classes are no better or worse than the English. Glenthorn's main business is to listen and learn, while the bright and sparkling Lady Geraldine reduces most of the guests to "mere puppets and parrots." "Mamma wants me to catch somebody, and to be caught by somebody," Geraldine remarks, "but that will not be; for, do you know, I think somebody is nobody" (*TN,* 4:280). Affable, candid, and opinionated, she is Irish and proud of being so, and the reader tends to share the high opinion she holds of her own judgments of others. The accomplishments of the silly Miss Tracey, who apes the fashions of fine people, are thus summed up by Geraldine: "She has a few notes nightingale, and all the rest rubbish" (*TN,* 4:281).

Lord Craiglethorpe, an English lord traveling about Ireland, is filled with English prejudices against Ireland and everything Irish. In her review of Carr's *The Stranger in Ireland,* Maria Edgeworth had criticized the peripatetic English tourist who judges a nation by a few isolated observations. In *Ennui,* Geraldine does the work for her by supplying Craiglethorp with "the most absurd anecdotes, incredible *facts,* stale jests, and blunders, such as were never made by true-born Irishmen" (*TN,* 4:287). Lord O'Toole, Lord Kilrush, and Captain Andrews, a trio of fashionable young men, may deceive others with inflated notions of their importance, but for Geraldine they are useful only as studies of intellectual shallowness and artifice. Geraldine's greatest ridicule, and the author's too, is reserved for Mrs. Norton and Lady Hauton, English ladies of no consequence in their own country, but a "prodigious *sensation*" in Ireland. The misguided belief that being somebody means slavish imitation of English manners, language, and dress is most fully exploited through Lady Clonbrony in *The Absentee.* In *Ennui* Lady Geraldine makes the point to her friends in a way not likely to be misunderstood: "Oh! my dear countrywomen, let us never stoop to admire and imitate these second-hand airs and graces, follies and vices. Let us dare to be ourselves!" (*TN,* 4:302).

If *Ennui* does not satisfactorily solve all the questions it raises, it is still important as the first full-scale picture of Irish society in fiction and the first serious study of Anglo-Irish landlordism.[33] Maria Edgeworth's contemporary critics were no more interested than the modern reader in the hero's neurosis or his romance. Jeffrey and Stephen must also have thumbed the beginning and ending chapters with amused if not short-tempered impatience, but what they found to praise were fresh discoveries about Irish life and society. They saw in Lady Geraldine an "enchantress with magic powers," a "half-wild, half-masculine, lofty and delicate character."[34] The Irish nurse Ellinor was also an original creation, a "most delectable personage" who combined "devoted affection, infantine simplicity, and strange pathetic eloquence."[35] The author herself was distinguished for "vivacity, knowledge of society, agreeable variety, and good writing."[36] When Jeffrey described the first series of *Tales of Fashionable Life* as being "actually as perfect as it was possible to make them,"[37] he had already singled out *Ennui* as his personal favorite.

The Absentee (1812)

On 30 August 1811, Maria wrote her cousin Sophy that she had just finished a little play called "The Absentee," a mixture of "comic and pathetic" which had met with favorable reception from the family's large juvenile audience. She doubted that the play would succeed on stage, and Sheridan answered her inquiry about it as she knew he would: under the prevailing circumstances, an English audience would be unlikely to sympathize with the distresses of the lower Irish, so vividly had she drawn them; and it would be impossible to find a cast who could "decently speak the Irish dialect for *so many Irish characters*."[38] At her father's suggestion she combined the unused Irish sequence omitted from *Patronage* with scenes from the play and, despite three weeks of violent toothache, finished the story and sent it off to the publisher in April 1812. It was, according to her stepmother, "less studied, less criticised, less corrected and more rapidly written than any other that Maria has published."[39]

The action of *The Absentee* falls naturally into three major phases, roughly equivalent to a three-act drama: the brilliant opening chapters that depict the Irish absentee Clonbrony family among the vulgar fashionable society of London; the central chapters, the longest and most interesting segment, in which the Clonbronys' only son, Lord Colambre, travels incognito to Ireland to learn more about the country and to view firsthand the management of his father's estates; and the closing chapters, which solve the problems that the story has raised. Colambre returns to England just in time to save his father from being ruined by the corrupt agent, Nicholas Garraghty. And he discovers that his beloved Grace Nugent is not only legitimate but an heiress as well. As the book ends, the Clonbrony family have arrived home to resume responsible management of their estates; preparations are being made for Colambre's marriage to Grace; and Larry, the Irish postilion, writes his brother that "it's growing the fashion not to be an Absentee" (*TN*, 6:264).

The opening scenes in which Lady Clonbrony succeeds in making herself ridiculous among the London fashionables are as good as anything of their kind in Maria Edgeworth's fiction. The method might be described, in Paulson's terms, as a "realism of presentation" as well as a "realism of assessment."[40] Lady Clonbrony is *"Henglish,* born in *Hoxfordshire,"* a product of deluded thinking that being somebody means being English. Her manners are a perfect butt for ridicule and satire, but her language is the chief source of her own apprehension "lest some treacherous *a* or *e,* some strong *r,* some puzzling aspirate or non-aspirate, some unguarded note, interrogative, or expostulatory, should betray her to be an Irish-woman" (*TN*, 6:5).

The costly preparations of the Clonbronys' London house for the gala affair—splendid reception rooms, Turkish tents, pagodas, Alhambra hangings, chalked mosaics—are in reality a prelude to increasing domestic misery and financial ruin. And while Lady Clonbrony caters to the leaders of the ton, the author's narrative voice makes us aware that the Lady Chattertons, Langdales, and Darevilles who attend "resolute not to admire" are no better than the object of their ridicule. We are at least made to sympathize with Lady Clonbrony, the outsider, while for the fashionable inside group we feel only contempt. And this is as it should be, for English fashionable society at large is the real object of the author's satire.

Lord Clonbrony realizes that if people would "stay in their own country, live on their own estates, and kill their own mutton, money need never be wanting" (*TN*, 6:20). A somebody in Ireland, he is a nobody in England, and to escape from his wife's wearisome friends, he finds solace in society that is beneath him. His major associate, and one of the book's most memorable characters, is Sir Terence O'Fay, to whose unreliable management Lord Clonbrony entrusts his business affairs. A jovial Irish profligate, O'Fay can tell a good story, sing a good song, or blunder the bull as well as anybody. Unfortunately, when Clonbrony takes him home, he appears to peculiar disadvantage.

In order to impress Colambre, a scholar fresh from Cambridge, and forward Mrs. Clonbrony's scheme to marry her son to Miss Broadhurst, O'Fay combines vague memories about gods and goddesses with other schoolboy scraps of knowledge for an original display of learning: "I hear great talk now of the Venus of Medici, and the Venus of this and that, with the Florence Venus, and the sable Venus, and that other Venus, that's washing of her hair . . . the golden Venus is the only one on earth that can stand . . . for gold rules the court, gold rules the camp, and men below, and heaven above" (*TN*, 6:23). The golden Venus is, of course, none other than Miss Broadhurst, whom the whole world expects Colambre to marry. O'Fay has special reason for urging Colambre's marriage to an heiress, for he has temporarily stalled an execution against the Clonbronys by the Jewish coachmaker, Mordicai. For Colambre, then, ending all doubts about his interest in Miss Broadhurst and determining reasons for his mother's dislike of Ireland are sufficient reasons for visiting the country.

Once across the Bay, Colambre meets the well-informed English soldier, Sir James Brooke, who explains the changes in Dublin society since the Union, a society in transition from the great houses to the rising middle classes. In the course of his journey, Colambre meets most of the classes that Brooke describes, so that the central chapters become a realistic rendering of post-Union Irish society. There is Mrs. Raffarty, the grocer's lady, with her little conservatory, pinery, grapery, and aviary, a representative of the tradesmen *pro tempore* class who begin without capital, buy and sell on credit, and follow every imaginable short-cut to fortune. Mrs. Raffarty's villa at Tusculum, a mixture of incongruity and taste, genius and absurdity, is matched by the lady herself, an exhibition of ignorance and affectation. As expected, then, her dinner that follows is a comic tour de force, matched only by Lady Clonbrony's earlier gala. Colambre makes the point, which is also the author's, that both ladies are actuated by the same desire, to appear what they are not.

In the town of Bray, Colambre meets Lady Dashfort and her daughter Isabel, affected English women, attempting to make a figure in Ireland. Dashfort offers to serve as Colambre's guide, but her motives are ulterior: she wants him to marry Isabel and settle in England. It is important, then, that he receive unfavorable impressions of Ireland, and to forward this scheme she introduces him to Kill-patricks-town, a survival of Gaelic Ireland into the nineteenth century. The atmosphere of *Castle Rackrent* hangs over Killpatricks-town where every day "one hundred and four people sit down to dinner" in a setting that is "sumptuous and unfinished" (*TN*, 6:103). Since Dashfort sets out "to select the worst instances, the worst exceptions" as examples "from which to condemn whole classes," we can hardly accept her views as the author's. Admittedly, the Killpatricks' lifestyle is not a pattern for imitation; but at least they have stayed with the land, and their treatment of the tenantry is more humane than the Garraghtys' on the Clonbrony estate. The Killpatricks form part of a social structure that also includes Count O'Halloran, a fine old Catholic soldier, and the Oranmores, idealized representations of the Anglo-Irish aristocracy.

O'Halloran's peculiarities individualize him as an interesting character, but his greater importance, as Flanagan suggests, may rest in what he symbolizes for Irish history: "a remnant of that Gaelic aristocracy which fled Ireland after Limerick to form the Irish brigades of France and the Irish regiments of Austria and Spain."[41] O'Halloran's study is populated by an eagle, a goat, and a greyhound, representatives of a past that few besides O'Halloran would understand. When O'Halloran moves the pets aside to make room for Colambre and his friends, Maria seems to speak for part of a nation's identity, as well as for a lonely survivor of a past now long since dead: "It was difficult to dislodge the old settlers, to make room for the new comers: but he adjusted these things with admirable facility; and, with a master's hand and a master's eye, compelled each favourite to retreat into the back settlements" (*TN*, 6:115). O'Halloran's strong negative attitudes about absenteeism help preserve the focus of the theme, as do the views of the Oranmores, whose example shows what can be done by resident proprietors.

Once arrived at his father's estates, Colambre, like Glenthorn before him, is presented with a vivid contrast between a good agent (Mr. Burke) and the vicious and unjust middlemen, Nick and Dennis Garraghty, managers of the larger portion of the estate. The proprietor of the inn describes the "good agent" as one who treats the tenants with justice, rewards them for improvements, and resides always on the land. What matters, as usual, is the relationship between landlord and tenant, and the proprietor's description, couched in the language of explanation, is a direct transcript from Edgeworth family history. Like M'Leod in *Ennui,* Burke runs a village school, attended by Protestants and Catholics, and like his predecessor, he is a model proprietor. The starkest scenes in the central chapters are reserved for Colambre's visit to Nugent's town, the setting of the Clonbronys' estates: "one row of miserable huts, sunk beneath the side of the road . . . all the roofs sunk in various places—thatch off, or overgrown with grass—no chimneys . . . dunghills before the doors, and green standing puddles—squalid children, with scarcely rags to cover them, gazing at the carriage" (*TN,* 6:144).

Nugent's town is undeniably a miserable spectacle, as are the lower Irish who inhabit it. Yet once there, we are less interested in the abstract speculations of Colambre than in the warm heart, quick wit, and generous impulse of Larry Brady, the Irish postilion. Through him we meet the rent pounders, the gauger, the informer, the exciseman, and the beggars; and because of him we remember long afterward the empty-eyed men and women standing in doorways of mud-walled cabins, bereft of energy and hope. Nick Garraghty's arrival in town precipitates a remarkable little scene at the inn, where Brannagan, the unlicensed proprietor, snatches whiskey from customers, clears the deck of patrons, and feigns illness, to stave off Old Nick. "Bad luck go with you, then!—and may you break your neck before you get home," Brannagan calls after him. And the reader's sympathies are with Brannagan all the way. The most famous scene, which Macaulay compared to the twenty-second book of the *Odyssey,*[42] occurs when Colambre interrupts Old Nick, on behalf of the poor O'Neil family, and reveals his identity to his tenantry and to their oppressor. The scene is handled in Maria Edgeworth's best dramatic manner, the interruption serving as a timely contrast between Garraghty's insolent injustice and the Widow's almost infantile simplicity and honesty. More important it signals an answer to the hero's question of personal and national identity; with his newly heightened social consciousness, he sees that his public responsibility belongs to his own country. The main problem is to convince his parents.

Back in London, Colambre saves his father from preying creditors and offers to dissolve his debts on condition that Garraghty be dismissed and the family return to Ireland. In a powerful and persuasive speech, Colambre pleads with his mother to return Lord Clonbrony "to his tenantry, his duties, his country, his home." Both parents are persuaded, and the ending—the novel's major weakness—is consumed almost entirely by the flimsy love story, the clearing of Grace

Nugent's family name so that the hero can marry her. Colambre's objection to Grace's supposed illegitimacy as an insurmountable obstacle to marriage not only reads prudishly but has little to do with the
theme. We see, of course, why Maria Edgeworth included it. It bears
the same relationship to *The Absentee* that Erasmus Percy's objection
to the daughter of a divorced mother bears to *Patronage:* the importance of the mother (echoes of Rousseau) in child rearing and the
larger influences of early environment in shaping character. Fortunately, the love story is incidental to the novel's larger accomplishments: a brilliant satire on universal foibles and follies, regardless of
time or place, and a serious study of the social and economic issues
of a national culture.

Ormond (1817)

The circumstances under which *Ormond* was composed are surely
among the most pathetic in literary history. Richard Lovell Edgeworth was dying, and Maria, with eyes swollen from exhaustion and
tears, longed to please her father in this, their final literary partnership. "Indeed," she wrote her brother and sister-in-law, "the wonderful exertions my father made sometimes working four or five hours
at a time correcting & dictating for me in his bed can only be conceived by those who know him and who saw him."[43] The novel was
written quickly but not hurriedly, and the author's distinction between the two is important: "There is a great deal of difference between writing rapidly and writing in a hurry—Whenever I have well
considered a subject, I think the more *rapidly* I write, the more likely
I am to preserve a unity of design & spirit through the whole."[44]
After *Castle Rackrent*, *Ormond* is often considered Maria Edgeworth's
best Irish novel, partly for the excellence of its design and partly for
a characteristic that her father ascribes to it in the preface: "The
moral of this tale does not immediately appear, for the author has
taken peculiar care that it should not obtrude itself upon the reader"
(*TN*, 9:iii).

The hero of the story is Harry Ormond, a warmhearted and impetuous young man, who was early abandoned by his father and
reared for a time in an Irish cabin by his mother. Following her
death, he is brought up by his father's friend, Sir Ulick O'Shane, an
affable and wily lord of Castle Hermitage, a member of the Irish Parliament, and a skillful intriguer in politics and public life. Ulick's

son Marcus is sent away to school and college, while Ormond, Ulick's real favorite, is allowed to "run wild" at home. All goes well until Ulick fears that Ormond will rival Marcus for the hand (and fortune) of Florence Annaly; and when in a shooting incident Ormond severely wounds the peasant, Moriarty Carroll, and insists on nursing him at Castle Hermitage, Ulick uses the incident as an excuse to send him off to the Black Islands, where Cornelius O'Shane, Ulick's cousin, is "King."

The opening chapters present a brilliant contrast between the cousins, representatives of two types of Irishmen. King Corny (Cornelius), a Catholic, lives a half-feudal, half-civilized existence on a remote, secluded island where the chief activities are hunting and fishing in an atmosphere of lawless freedom. It is not surprising that Corny, who loves Ormond as his "own soul," would send for him in a "six-oared boat, streamers flying, and piper playing like mad" or that a ragged multitude, following Corny's example, would greet the young man as "Prince Harry." Ormond has lived in Ulick's public world long enough to realize that his boyhood views of Corny were colored by the magic of a child's imagination, that Corny then appeared to him as the greatest, the richest, and most ingenious of men. For had Corny not made a rattrap and a violin with his own hands? And boots, and hat, and coat, and shoes and stockings—were they not all the best because Corny had made them? But now he begins to question if some things might not be more usefully made by tradesmen— the violin, for example—with less time and trouble. And Corny's energy, genius, and perseverance might be better spent on greater objects.

It is natural that Corny should despise Ulick, an apostate Anglo-Irishman, who bends easily in an effort to be all things to all men. Ulick's unexpected visit to the Black Islands, soon after Ormond's arrival, is a beautifully orchestrated scene in which Ulick and Corny rip apart old grievances, attacking and parrying in tones of muted hatred and grudging respect. Corny begins the attack. There is the matter of Ulick's baronetage which must have cost a pretty penny in conscience and money; and Ulick's speculating in silver mines, useless prospecting; and Ulick's breaking the heart of poor Emmy Annaly, his first wife, under the pretense of being a reformed rake.

Ulick's retorts are likewise filled with smoke and sparks. Corny's outmoded farming equipment loses money in wasted time; and Corny's unique ploughing team (a bull, a mule, and two lean horses) are more occupied in eating their rope harnesses than in ploughing; and there is Corny's feudal notion about renovating a castle from the roof down. According to Corny, the problem with Ulick is that he "woodcocks—hides his head, and forgets his body can be seen." The term perfectly suits the man and his visit, for Ulick fears that Lady Annaly's letter to Ormond (which Ulick delivers) has something to do with Ormond and Florence Annaly. Fortunately, for Ulick, the letter is a harmless list of Ormond's faults which the young man carelessly dropped under a tree. "Woodcocked!" Corny says after Ulick's departure, "if ever man did, by all that's cunning!" (*TN,* 9:280).

Corny attempts to make Ormond understand that Ulick is jealous of his rivaling the son Marcus. The idea is inconceivable to Ormond, who sees himself as a raw, uninformed, and ignorant boy without education or fortune. And so he is for a time. Yet Ormond is blessed with natural genius (which Richard Lovell Edgeworth no longer denies) and with simple nobility that improves with time and experience. Central to the action of the plot is Ormond's ability to grow and change for the better through experience—not only through the influence of the company he keeps at Castle Hermitage, in the Black Islands, in Dublin, and in Paris, but also through the influence of his reading. The skillful rendering of the effects of reading on a fictional character's growth may be, as Norman Jeffares suggests, a new development in the novel.[45]

Ormond is attracted by the wit and humor of *Tom Jones* and sees in the character of the hero, "a warm-hearted, generous, imprudent young man . . . governed more by feeling than by principle," a resemblance to his own. Since he now resolves to "shine forth an Irish Tom Jones," he does not feel "at all bound to be a moral gentleman" or "a *gentleman* at all." With his "head full of Tom Jones," he almost succumbs to the temptation of seducing Peggy Sheridan, the gardener's daughter. But when he discovers that Moriarty is in love with her and that his own folly has almost broken Moriarty's heart, he is cured of the Jones mania, and later helps Moriarty marry her. Through Lady Annaly's present of books, Ormond is next introduced to Richardson and discovers in the character of Sir Charles Grandison a model that "inspired him with virtuous emulation, and made him ambitious to be a *gentleman* . . . in short, it completely counteracted in his mind the effects of his late study" (*TN,* 9:294). In Maria Edgeworth's judgment, Tom Jones and Sir Charles Grandison are both attractive heroes; her purpose, of course, is to show that Ormond's learning process is enlarged by the contrasts he sees between them as fictional characters and the comparisons he makes between them and the "friends he loved in real life." So much for the effect of reading on his nascent mind, but the reflective principles must now be tested.

The coming of spring will herald the return of Corny's pretty daughter Dora who, accompanied by her Aunt, Mlle O'Faley, has been away studying with a dancing master. Corny has warned Ormond that Dora must be considered as good as married because of Corny's allegiance to an outmoded code of honor. Before she was born, Corny promised Dora in marriage to the eldest son of a neighbor, a dispossessed gentleman of old Irish stock. And although Corny eventually wishes that the "unlucky bowl of punch had remained for ever unmixed," he is true to his word. With touching boyish innocence, Ormond looks forward to Dora's arrival, for she can teach him dancing, drawing, and French, and improve his manners. As it turns out, she teaches him none of these things, but what he discovers about her character is important to his learning process.

It is clear that she cares nothing for White Conal, who, as Corny discovers too late, is a "purse-proud grazier and mean man—not a remnant of a gentleman! as the father was" (*TN*, 9:325). Why, then, would she marry him? Fortunately for Dora, White Conal is killed in a fall from a horse, but Black Conal, his twin brother, remains. Black Conal dazzles Dora with a grandiose representation of Parisian life and, with a brilliant talent for conversation, gratifies her vanity through flattery. Ormond sees what Dora fails to see—that Conal is a fortune-seeking coxcomb without delicacy and feeling. In selecting Conal over Ormond (assisted partly by her aunt's trickery), Dora also opts for a way of life that offers little happiness. She realizes this later, but the choice itself establishes a moral landscape in the novel that also includes Ormond.

Corny is killed in a hunting accident, and Ormond, true to his promise, places the body in the coffin, attends the wake, and joins the crowded concourse of people in the three-mile journey to the remote old burial ground. As they pass the doors of cabins, women raise the funeral cry—"not a savage howl . . . but chanting a melancholy kind of lament, not without harmony, simple and pathetic" (*TN*, 9:374). Ormond is convinced that the poor people mourn sincerely for the friend they have lost. Following the funeral, Ormond accepts the invitation of Dr. Cambray, a benevolent Anglican clergyman, to reside at Vicar's Dale. He is not here long when Sir Ulick returns to claim his ward—and with good reason, since with the death of his Indian stepmother, Ormond has inherited an impressive fortune. Naturally eager to patronize a young man in prosperity, Ulick cautiously agrees to split Ormond's time between Castle Hermitage and Vicar's Dale.

At Castle Hermitage, Ormond is reintroduced to public life and to "late dinners, and long dinners, and great dinners, fine plate, good dishes, and plenty of wine, but a dearth of conversation—the natural topics chained up by etiquette" (TN, 9:400). Almost ensnared by an imprudent young lady, Ormond decides to tour Ireland, but noticeably absent from his journey are the fresh, vigorous scenes of *Ennui* and *The Absentee*. This is perhaps as it should be, since Glenthorn and Colambre viewed the country as outsiders, and to avoid an English tourist kind of misinterpretation it was necessary that they receive a panoramic view of the country. As a native of Ireland Ormond travels for a different reason, to improve himself by meeting cultured and well-bred people.

As it turns out, what he learns has largely to do with Sir Ulick and, as always, with himself. Ulick is well-known in the country—so well, in fact, that his private jobbing and public defection of principle have become subjects of puns, epigrams, and songs, newly published in a collected edition. Ormond's defense of Ulick (to the extent of fighting a duel with a spirited young man) says more about Ormond's character than about Ulick's reputation. It is Ormond's allegiance to a guardian who rescued an orphan boy from a smoky cabin and placed him in a childhood paradise called Castle Hermitage. Nevertheless, stories about the duel and gossip about Ormond reach Lady Annaly, and Ormond is gratified by an invitation to visit the Annalys on his route homeward.

The English-educated Annalys rise steadily in Ormond's esteem, and what he learns from them is important to the course of his future life. The real moment of truth for Ormond—and partly for Maria Edgeworth, too—comes during a visit to Sir Herbert Annaly's estate when the hero compares the Annaly and O'Shane modes of estate management. Herbert Annaly, like M'Leod *(Ennui)* and Burke *(The Absentee)*, is the model proprietor whose watchwords are justice and humanity. And it is Herbert Annaly whom Ormond chooses as a landlord model. Sir Ulick, like Sir Murtagh *(Castle Rackrent)* and

Nick and Dennis Garraghty *(The Absentee)*, governs by threats and punishments, bribery and abuse; and Ulick's bigoted son Marcus, like his predecessor Hardcastle *(Ennui)*, believes that tenants must be deceived and enslaved.

In temperament, Herbert Annaly resembles Corny, but whereas Corny's ruling passion was generosity, Herbert's is justice. Ormond admits that his heart leans toward Corny and his head toward Annaly, but the two might be reconciled through justice when exercised with prudence. Since in the Irish context justice is a peculiarly English virtue, it is fitting that Ormond and Florence should be drawn together by a mutual desire for justice. The Catholic child, Tommy Dunshaughlin, receives the scholarship despite intervention from the English Protestant bigot, Mrs. M'Crule; but in pursuing her own hatred, she has served the interests of Ormond's love.

Or so it seems. Ormond proposes to Florence much too hastily, and the confusion that follows causes him to doubt her sincerity. For this reason, he accepts the Conals' invitation to visit Paris. The Parisian scenes (influenced by Richard Lovell Edgeworth's French visit in 1773 and by the family visit in 1802) are as excellent in their way as the Irish. Ormond is introduced to a broad cross-section of French society, a brilliant and dazzling array of people and places set in the latter years of Louis XV. Mlle O'Faley, once described by Ulick as "that thing half Irish, half French, half mud, half tinsel," is now in ecstasy. But Ormond is most astonished by Dora, by how quickly an Irish country girl has been metamorphosed into a beautiful French woman of fashion. It was spring in the Black Islands when Dora accepted Black Conal and the promise of a life of splendor. Spring is now coming to Paris, where Dora confronts her moment of truth: "Oh! Harry, my first, my best, my only friend, I have enjoyed but little real happiness since we parted" *(TN,* 9:500). It is here, too, in the spring, that Ormond meets Marmontel, whose example reminds him of virtue and domestic life—and of Florence Annaly and a choice different from Dora's—and turns his thoughts toward home.

On hearing that Ulick's bank is failing, Ormond leaves immediately for London and arrives just in time to save most of his own fortune. But the bank collapses, and Ormond reaches Castle Hermitage to find Ulick "dead . . . and cold, and in his coffin." The contrast between the quiet and secret funeral of Sir Ulick and the earlier magnificent ceremony of King Corny is obvious to the poor people who are allowed to draw their own moral: "They compared him with King Corny, and 'see the difference!' said they; 'the one was the *true thing, and never changed*—and after all, where is the great friends now? . . . See, with all his wit, and the schemes upon schemes, broke and gone, and forsook and forgot, and buried without a funeral, or a tear, but from Master Harry' " (*TN,* 9:520). Ormond agrees with their simple and just evaluation. Faced with a choice of buying Castle Hermitage (the better bargain) or the Black Islands, Ormond chooses the Black Islands. And in marrying Florence Annaly, he combines English reliability with Irish warmth of heart, common to both Corny and Ulick, to whom, all along, he is heir in spirit.

Maria's brother Sneyd thought *Ormond* superior to anything else she had written,[46] and even if we do not agree, the reasons for thinking it so are not hard to find. Glenthorn and Colambre were both aliens whose learning was restricted largely to discoveries about Ireland. While the half-English, half-Irish Ormond is not formally educated, he is more capable than either of understanding what he learns. At first, Glenthorn is something of an English dandy, and Colambre— certainly in all that has to do with his romance—is a prig. Ormond begins as a sensitive and lovable boy whose growth into manhood is a carefully detailed process of self-discovery. What he learns, of course, involves three national cultures; and in this sense, as Butler points out, Maria Edgeworth's early and extended use of an international theme makes her an important precursor to Henry James.[47] Unlike Glenthorn and Colambre, Ormond is not used as a critic or, in Emily Lawless's words, as a "peg to hang edifying sentiments upon."[48] The novel, in fact, shares the same relationship with the Irish fiction that *Helen* shares with the English works, for both are a final reconciliation of heart and head; and since heart predominates, *Ormond,* like *Helen,* is the fullest expression of Maria Edgeworth herself.

Irish nationalist critics would not agree. "For all that gave significance and value to the history of the Irish Celt," Stephen Gwynn writes, "for all his heritage from the past, she cared nothing."[49] *Ormond* tells us differently. If the hero decides to model himself on a modern-minded Annaly, he does so because the Annaly way of life is more just, because the Annaly system of landlord management is more humane. And if he marries an Annaly, he selects her from competition that includes young women in France, as well as England. In truth, the rational English folk—the Annalys and Cam-

brays—finally have very little to do in the novel and as characters are
not very important except as occasional reminders of the straight and
narrow. There are some finely realized minor characters—Mrs.
M'Crule, Moriarty, Mlle O'Faley. But the book belongs to the
O'Shanes who share with Thady Quirk the distinction of being Maria
Edgeworth's most brilliant Irish characters.

Sir Ulick embodies all the striking ambivalencies of Irish character
at its best: cunning, deceit, generosity, shrewdness, deference, audac-
ity, conviviality, talismanic charm. But it is Corny, the old Gaelic
proprietor, who provides the lyric touches; it is the spirit of Corny,
even after his death, that pervades the book, that provides the story's
great moments. The moment, for instance, after Corny's death, when
Ormond and Moriarty walk along the lone heath-bog and discover
the letters that Moriarty had cut in the earth a year before—"Long
Live King Corny"—sprouting now with broomcorn in the spring.
The moment when Ormond visits his little farm in the Black Islands,
the gift from Corny, for a renewal of spirits before he leaves for the
mainland of Ireland. The moment in Paris when Dora's ring (adorned
with her father's hair) reminds them of another spring in the Black
Islands and of "that fond father, that generous benefactor, that confiding friend" (*TN*, 9:501). Or the moment of crucial decision when
Ormond purchases the Black Islands and decides to return to a people
who "offered up prayers for his coming again" (*TN*, 9:528).

Neither *Ormond* nor *Helen* attempts solutions to the human predicament, but both end on a note of acceptance and hope. The spirit of
Maria Edgeworth's last Irish novel suggests that Lady Davenant's advice to Helen would do for Ormond as well: "We must take people
as they are; you may graft a rose upon an oak, but those who have
tried the experiment tell us the graft will last but a short time, and
the operation ends in the destruction of both" (*TN*, 10:51).

Chapter Six
Maria Edgeworth's Achievement

"Whereas Jane Austen was so much the better novelist Maria Edgeworth may be the more important."[1] Newby's perceptive observation is a coinage in Edgeworth criticism, but the statement needs expanding to make sense. It is not news that Jane Austen is a better technician than Maria Edgeworth, but whereas Austen lacked disciples, Maria Edgeworth's influence on nineteenth-century literature was pronounced. At the same time, it must be acknowledged that her importance is much more than historical.

Any sound estimate of her achievement must begin with genre, for the range of her writings is truly impressive, and what she attempted was often as important as what she achieved. Education was, of course, at the forefront of her consciousness. And as educational theorists, she and her father were, in Desmond Clarke's words, "more than a century ahead of their time."[2] Their attempt to understand the psychology of childhood and learning, their concern for individual differences, their condemnation of rote learning and outmoded curricula, and their belief that education included much more than simple instruction and textbook learning—all are accepted as commonplaces today. Yet at least two educationists in this century believe that the source of nineteenth-century educational reform has wrongly been attributed to Pestalozzi and that those who appreciate the Edgeworths' grasp of child nature may "wonder why English people at any rate have given all the honour for the discovery of the child to any and everyone save their own countryman."[3] We remember the author's claim for her father as having been the first to practice the experimental method in education.

Throughout her father's lifetime, Maria Edgeworth viewed fiction as entertainment combined with instruction and believed that her tales and novels would best promote her father's educational theories. Her attitude toward fiction was not at all unusual to an age when a writer was expected to provide much more than a faithful imitation of reality; there must also be concern for education and strict control of moral influence. Her preoccupation with educational theory was at once a key to the strengths and weaknesses of her fiction. Her most emphatic theme is the contrast between reality—what people and society are like—and illusion—the way we choose to know them. And basic to this theme was the belief she shared with her father, that only through education do we understand the nature and use of reality.

Throughout her literary career, she recognized that the "morals" of her stories were sometimes too prominent. For instance, in response to Mrs. Inchbald's criticism of *Patronage,* she confessed, "To the good of our moral we were obliged to sacrifice; perhaps we have sacrificed in vain."[4] Interestingly enough, she was her own severest critic, and her revealing letters suggest that she was fully aware of her deficiencies in plot construction. Yet it might be admitted that her use of instructive antitheses and her commitment to poetic justice are the pitfalls of any fiction writer whose primary mission is to teach.

Her desire to teach, on the other hand, undoubtedly contributed to her significance and stature as a writer. That she was the first classic writer for children has never been disputed, even by historians of the novel. "Miss Edgeworth's is so entirely the child's point of view," E. A. Baker remarks, "that she merely seems to the puzzled infant mind to be making things beautifully clear and showing exactly how it is that effects are determined by causes."[5] Equally important is her influence on later writers for children. Vineta Colby speaks of "the intangible but profound influence of her tales for children upon the developing consciousness of the major Victorian novelists." In Colby's view, "all the little Jane Eyres and David Copperfields and Maggie Tullivers and Richard Feverels were pupils in the schoolroom of the 'education of the heart,' for which Maria Edgeworth . . . [was] supplying curricula and texts."[6] Luisa-Teresa Unthank, on the other hand, suggests thematic parallels between her stories and those of more recent writers such as Dorothy Clewes (*Library Lady,* 1971) and singer Julie Andrews (*Mandy,* 1971). In addition, Unthank notes that her method of testing the effectiveness of her stories by the judgments of child critics has also been used by the modern educational psychologist and writer, Jean Piaget.[7]

Maria Edgeworth's tales and novels for women—indeed, her attitudes toward women—have often been misunderstood in this cen-

tury. For in identifying ourselves with such heroines as Caroline
(*Letters for Literary Ladies*), Belinda (*Belinda*), and Leonora (*Leonora*)—
"so rational, so prudent, so well-behaved, so replete with solid information," as Bulwer Lytton described them—we have failed to
recognize the emerging pattern of values in the fiction as a whole. In
chapter 3 we have seen that the fiction for women is at once a dramatization and reconciliation of the conflicting claims of the "head" and
"heart," and by both terms the author meant something quite specific. She believed that the "head" must be rationally educated, since
sexual equality could only be realized through education. And if she
did not campaign publicly for women's rights, she quietly challenged
women all along in her fiction to accept their right to self-realization.
One theme in her fiction for women, as Butler points out, is "opposition to that upper-class herd-instinct that expects unthinking con-
formism to a received view."[8] For this reason, the contrast between
her own and Jane Austen's attitudes toward women must surely seem
significant to the modern reader.

In stressing the importance of the individual, Maria Edgeworth
diverges from conservative advocates of sense. And as Butler suggests,
the "characteristic recourse of the conservative—Burke, Jane West,
Jane Austen—is to remind us ultimately of the insignificance of individual insights and even individual concerns when measured against
the scale of the 'universe as one vast whole.' "[9] In terms of society,
Jane Austen's heroines must understand what action is possible. For
Maria Edgeworth, social approval is not generally condoned; her heroines are less interested in catching husbands than in seeking knowledge, integrity, and self-fulfillment.

Yet an equally important theme—dramatized brilliantly in *Belinda*
and developed most fully in *Helen*—is the education of the heart, the
cultivation of the temper, emotions, and instincts. "We shall never
learn to feel and respect our real calling and destiny," Scott said during his Irish visit in 1825, "unless we have taught ourselves to consider everything as moonshine, compared with the education of the
heart."[10] It is understandable why Maria Edgeworth disliked Belinda
and Leonora as heroines, for neither expressed her own character and
personality. Fortunately, Lady Delacour (*Belinda*) and Helen (*Leonora*)
do the work for her, as do Cecilia, Helen, and Lady Davenant in
Helen. All of them (and Griselda and Mrs. Beaumont, too) disprove
the traditional view that she is stuffily edifying, for they clearly demonstrate that principles (esteem, duty, honor, gratitude) are not in

themselves sufficient to happiness. Feeling and emotion are equally important, and for this reason Maria Edgeworth, like Scott, stands about midway in the spectrum which Jane Austen called "Sense and Sensibility."

In *Vivian, Patronage,* and *Harrington,* the author's attention shifted, as we have seen, from "female" concerns to public issues and to roles that men play in public life—matters that do not come remotely within the range of anything that Burney or Austen attempted. As Butler points out, she developed in these (and in the Irish) novels "a connection never before consciously made in the novel, the economic connection between an individual and his wider social context."[11] While *Patronage* is structurally the weakest of the three novels, it is perhaps the clearest expression of an individual's need for both moral and intellectual independence as preparation for public life. And the character of Lord Oldborough fully dramatizes the public life of a man whose importance depends on his uses of power. Oldborough *(Patronage)* and Glistonbury *(Vivian)* remind us of Watson's observation that Maria Edgeworth "steals a long march over Jane Austen in the credibility of her male characters."[12]

Historians of the novel generally agree that the social novel originated with Fanny Burney and that Maria Edgeworth converted it into a permanent form. For this reason, she formed a bridge between the novel of the eighteenth century and that of the nineteenth. We know that she freely borrowed the format of *Evelina* for *Belinda* and that most of the themes of her English fiction were commonplace in the eighteenth-century novel—the lost heir, for instance, or the accidental reversal of fortune, or the inevitably happy union of eligible young ladies and gentlemen. Yet if her plots were often neither original nor well constructed, her English novels still deserve our attention—not only for their memorable gallery of characters, but for techniques that still seem peculiarly modern today.

Maria Edgeworth is a gifted delineator of character, and it is probably safe to predict that Lady Delacour *(Belinda)* and Lady Davenant *(Helen)* will never be surpassed—the one, convinced that she is dying, feared and envied but unloved, conscience-stricken, afraid that she is losing her senses; the other, magisterial, yet human, a resolute mind of affairs, and the first of her type in fiction. Griselda ("The Modern Griselda") and Mrs. Beaumont ("Manoeuvring") are smaller stars in the galaxy, but all of them (and the list could be greatly expanded) shine brightly because they live as beings in the mind of their creator. Scott spoke of her "formidable powers of acute observation."[13] And Jane Austen's judgment of *Belinda* is well known: a "work in which the greatest powers of the mind are displayed, in which the most thorough knowledge of human nature, the happiest delineation of its varieties, the liveliest effusions of wit and humour, are conveyed to the world in the best chosen language" *(Northanger Abbey, chapter 5).*

Maria Edgeworth's versatility in using language to reveal character—from the simple language of children in *The Parent's Assistant* to the polished, sophisticated dialogue of her fashionables, to the authoritative speech of her men in public life, to the vernacular of her Irish natives—has generally been recognized. But what is surely as important is her impressive understanding of the psychology of human behavior, the internal and external forces that motivate people to act the way they do. Without her father's intrinsic interest in the relationship of mind to behavior, it is doubtful that her absorbing studies of human psychology in *Vivian, Harrington,* and *Helen* would have been written at all. Dickens's Pip and David Copperfield may have profited from her young Harrington, who attempts to understand the person he is by exploring the childhood experience that scarred his psyche. *Helen* (which suggested the plot for Frederika Bremer's *A Diary* and for a portion of Mrs. Gaskell's *Wives and Daughters*) is her fullest exploration of consciousness. Walter Allen includes her—along with Richardson, Smollett, and Dickens—as a user of the stream-of-consciousness technique.[14] Not only does the third volume of *Helen* contain instances of "impassioned self-scrutiny," but the author's narrative voice is entirely absent for impressive periods of time.

Maria Edgeworth's literary reputation today rests almost entirely on her Irish fiction. And because of principles that are peculiar to modern criticism, *Castle Rackrent* is now the best-known and most widely read of her four studies of Irish life. This was not, of course, the case during her lifetime; her own critics and reviewers were equally impressed by her authentic portrayals of Irish life and society in *Ennui, The Absentee,* and *Ormond,* and despite her flaws in plotting, they shared a consensus: that when her subject was Irish, Maria Edgeworth was the best and most important writer of her time. One reviewer's remarks are not only complimentary, but typical: "We never saw the Irish grouped—we never trode [*sic*] with them on Irish ground—we never viewed them as natives of a kindred soil, surrounded by the atmosphere of home, and all those powerful accessaries [*sic*] which made *them* natural, and *us* comparatively strange and foreign. We had seen them alone in English crowds—solitary foreigners, brought over to amuse us with their peculiarities, but we had never been carried to Ireland, and made familiar with them by their own hearths, till, for the first time, they were shown to us by Miss Edgeworth."[15]

Critics and historians of the novel generally agree that Maria Edgeworth's Irish fiction exerted important influence on the subsequent course of the novel. *Rackrent,* for example, is considered the first regional novel and the first serious treatment of the Irish peasantry in fiction; it is one of the earliest family-history chronicles, tracing the history of a family through several generations; and, as Watson points out, it is the "first consistent attempt to compose a novel in any dialect of English."[16] Thackeray most likely borrowed the device of transparency in *Rackrent* for his own autobiography of *Barry Lyndon;* and this is not surprising since he knew the work well and praised it highly.[17]

Although Thady Quirk is the most brilliant character sketch that the author ever drew, it is probable, as Butler suggests, that *Ennui, The Absentee,* and *Ormond* were more influential on the subsequent development of the novel.[18] They are accurately observed studies of a nation's culture and people, the first serious examinations in fiction of the workings of a social, political, and economic system. Scott openly admitted that he tried to do for Scotland what Maria Edgeworth had done for Ireland. And Cooper (in *The Spy*) and Turgenev (in *Memoirs of a Sportsman*) are generally thought to have been indebted to her example. The Irish novelists Lover, Lever, Carleton, and Banim cultivated a field that she had planted; and in 1845, only four years before her death, Lever dedicated his *Tom Burke* to her, the first, he said, "in my country's literature."[19]

If Maria Edgeworth had not made substantial contributions to the literature of education and pedagogy; if she had not been an important writer of children's stories that were read by generations and served as models for the genre; and if she had not exerted pronounced influence on the development of prose fiction, the "great Maria"—as Scott called her—would still be worth reading as a novelist. No longer can Ruskin's judgment—that "all Miss Edgeworth has ever written is eternal and classic literature—of the eternal as much as Carlyle—as much as Homer"—be read without surprise.[20] But that it could be said at all is a measure not only of her influence but also of her power. Both give us some idea of the place that Maria Edgeworth ought to have in the history of the English and Anglo-Irish novel.

Notes and References

Chapter One

1. Maria Edgeworth (ME) to Sophy Ruxton, 18 October 1796. Appended note by Richard Lovell Edgeworth (RLE). References to individual letters are from family manuscripts. See bibliography.

2. Rowland Grey, "Maria Edgeworth and Etienne Dumont," *Dublin Review* 145 (1909):256.

3. I have followed traditional practice in Edgeworth scholarship by referring to the author as Maria and to her father as Edgeworth.

4. Richard Lovell Edgeworth and Maria Edgeworth, *Memoirs of Richard Lovell Edgeworth* (1820; reprint, Shannon, 1968), 1:15 ff.

5. ME's birth date is commonly assumed to be 1767. For this revised date, see Butler and Colvin, "A Revised Date of Birth for Maria Edgeworth," under secondary sources in the bibliography.

6. Frances Ann Edgeworth, *A Memoir of Maria Edgeworth* (London, 1867), 1:1.

7. RLE to ME, Great Berkhamstead, 1778.

8. *The Education of the Heart: The Correspondence of Rachel Mordecai Lazarus and Maria Edgeworth,* ed. Edgar E. MacDonald (Chapel Hill, 1977), 175.

9. Edgeworth and Edgeworth, *Memoirs,* 2:iv.

10. These details form the basis of Glenthorn's experience with the Irish tenantry in *Ennui.* See chapter 5.

11. ME used her father's experience, as described here, as a foundation for the practices of her model landlords in *Ennui, The Absentee,* and *Ormond.* See chapter 5.

12. Edgeworth and Edgeworth, *Memoirs,* 2:32.

13. Edgeworth, *Memoir,* 1:143.

14. *Maria Edgeworth: Letters From England, 1813–1844,* ed. Christina Colvin (Oxford, 1971), 59.

15. Ibid., 51.

16. Byron's "Ravenna Journal," 19 January 1821, in *Byron's Letters and Journals,* ed. Leslie A. Marchand (Cambridge, 1978), 8:30.

17. ME to Mrs. Margaret Ruxton, June (?) 1817.

18. *Maria Edgeworth,* ed Colvin, 15.

19. Frances Beaufort to ME, 1798.

20. Fragment, probably to Mrs. F. E. Edgeworth, August 1802 (?).

21. P. H. Newby, *Maria Edgeworth* (Denver, 1950), 18.

22. According to *A Memoir of Maria Edgeworth* (2:7), RLE's passages include the death of King Corny which closes chapter 14 of *Ormond*. The passage is one of the most moving scenes in the novel. ME herself did not remember most of her father's passages, but for his other probable interpolations and excisions, see Patrick Murray, "Maria Edgeworth and Her Father: The Literary Partnership," *Eire* 6 (1971):39–50.

23. 5 December 1812.

24. Marilyn Butler, *Maria Edgeworth: A Literary Biography* (Oxford, 1972), 271–304.

25. Ibid., 288.

26. Edgeworth, *Memoir*, 3:77.

27. RLE's unpopularity also exerted a marked negative influence on ME's later career. See Butler, *Maria Edgeworth*, 412–13.

28. *Education of the Heart*, ed. MacDonald, 275–76.

29. Ibid., 288.

30. Edgeworth, *Memoir*, 3:259.

Chapter Two

1. F. J. Harvey Darton says that with the advent of Maria Edgeworth, "a new kind of writer for children is appearing" since she was thinking of "real children, not of hypostatized moral qualities." See *Children's Books in England* (1932; reprint, London, 1960), 144–45. See also *A Critical History of Children's Literature*, ed. Cornelia Meigs et al. (New York, 1953), 103–5.

2. Edgeworth, *Memoir*, 1:95. Criticism stemmed mainly from the authors' omission of religious education. For over fifteen years critics and reviewers used the omission to discredit both the fiction and the educational works. See Butler, *Maria Edgeworth*, 341–42.

3. Brian Simon, *Studies in the History of Education* (London, 1960), 25.

4. Alice Paterson, *The Edgeworths: A Study of Later Eighteenth Century Education* (London, 1914), v–vi.

5. Maria Edgeworth and Richard Lovell Edgeworth, *Practical Education* (Boston, 1823), 449; hereafter cited in the text as *PE*.

6. Since no copy of the 1795 edition of *The Parent's Assistant* has been located, the dates of the stories are uncertain (see Butler, *Maria Edgeworth*, 159). *Early Lessons* (1801–25), ME's other major work for children, is a series of instructive dialogues designed to teach rational and secular principles of behavior through object lessons.

7. The 1796 edition probably included "Lazy Lawrence," "The False Key," "Mademoiselle Panache" (continued in *Moral Tales*), "The Mimic," "The Birthday Present," "The Bracelets," "Tarlton," "The Barring Out," and "Old Poz" (a play).

8. "Simple Susan," "The Little Merchants," "Eton Montem" (a play), "The Basket Woman," "Waste Not, Want Not," "Forgive and Forget," "The White Pigeon," and "The Orphans."

9. F. J. Harvey Darton, "Children's Books," in *Cambridge History of English Literature* (New York, 1917), 11:423.

10. Newby, *Maria Edgeworth*, 24.

11. Mary Hill Arbuthnot, *Children and Books*, 3d ed. (Glenview, Ill., 1964), 42. See also Jane Bingham and Grayce Scholt, *Fifteen Centuries of Children's Literature: An Annotated Chronology of British and American Works in Historical Context* (Westport, Conn., 1980), 129.

12. Darton, *Children's Books in England*, 53.

13. Ibid., 164.

14. Darton, "Children's Books," 11:424.

15. For the relationship between the child figure in children's literature and the concept of a fallen universe, see Robert Pattison, *The Child Figure in English Literature* (Athens, Ga., 1978), 135–59.

16. From Gillian Avery, *Childhood's Patterns: A Study of the Heroes and Heroines of Children's Fiction, 1770–1950* (London, 1975), 97.

17. Annie E. Moore, *Literature Old and New For Children: Materials for a College Course* (Cambridge, 1934), 203–4.

18. ME's other fiction for adolescents includes "The Mental Thermometer" (1801; probably written when the author was sixteen) and "Orlandino" (1848; a temperance story written for the Irish Relief Fund).

19. ME to Letty Ruxton, 29 January 1800. The *Moral Tales* include "The Good Aunt," "The Good French Governess," "Mademoiselle Panache," "Forester," "Angelina," "The Prussian Vase," and "The Knapsack" (a play).

20. Francis Jeffrey, review of *Popular Tales*, *Edinburgh Review* 4 (1804):337.

21. Maria Edgeworth, *Tales and Novels*, Longford Edition (1893; reprint, Georg Olms Verlagsbuchhandlung, 1969), 1:281; hereafter cited in the text as *TN*. All references to the tales and novels except *Castle Rackrent* are from this edition.

22. The *Popular Tales* include "Lame Jervas," "The Will," "The Limerick Gloves," "Out of Debt Out of Danger," "The Lottery," "Rosanna," "Murad the Unlucky," "The Manufacturers," "The Contrast," "The Grateful Negro," and "To-Morrow."

23. J. M. S. Tompkins, *The Popular Novel in England, 1770–1800* (Lincoln, 1961), 72.

Chapter Three

1. Edgeworth, *Memoir*, 3:266.

2. ME to Sophy Ruxton, November 1803.

3. "Letter of Maria Edgeworth to Mr. Hunter," *Notes and Queries* 12 (23 June 1923):488.

4. Edgeworth, *Memoir*, 1:229–30.

5. Marilyn Butler, *Jane Austen and the War of Ideas* (Oxford, 1975), 141.

6. Walter Allen, *The English Novel* (New York, 1958), 113.

7. ME to Sophy Ruxton, November 1803.

8. Edgeworth and Edgeworth, *Memoirs*, 2:353.

9. Butler, *Jane Austen*, 152.

10. Mark D. Hawthorne, *Doubt and Dogma in Maria Edgeworth* (Gainesville, 1967), 63.

11. Clara Reeve, *The School for Widows* (London, 1791), 1:vi.

12. ME to Mrs. Ruxton, 3 November 1803.

13. ME to Margaret Ruxton, 13 March 1809.

14. ME to Charlotte Sneyd (ME's aunt), 19 November 1808.

15. ME to Sophy Ruxton, December 1808.

16. Edgeworth, *Memoir*, 3:142.

17. Ibid., 3:79.

18. Butler, *Maria Edgeworth*, 459.

19. Edgeworth, *Memoir*, 3:84.

20. Lady Davenant is responsible for Cecilia's flawed education: "talents should make themselves objects of Love not fear." See Butler, *Maria Edgeworth*, 476.

Chapter Four

1. ME to Sophy Ruxton, Edgeworthstown, 26 February 1805.

2. RLE to ME, 1805.

3. Richard Lovell Edgeworth, *Essays on Professional Education*, 2d ed. (London, 1812), 37. In the preface to this edition, RLE resolutely disclaims "the opinion, that boys should be bred up from their infancy by conversation, instruction, and books *exclusively* adapted to peculiar professions" (v–vi), a response, most likely, to harsh reviews of the earlier edition. ME's fiction makes at least two responses: Glistonbury's ideas about training his son (*Vivian*, 5:257) parody the whole concept of professional training during infancy; and Alfred Percy's faith in early liberal education in *Patronage* (see this chapter) suggests a more balanced view.

4. ME to Sophy Ruxton, 23 January 1808.

5. ME to Mrs. Ruxton, 1810 (?).

6. ME to Charles Sneyd Edgeworth (ME's half brother), May 1812.

7. ME to Mrs. Ruxton, 2 February 1809.

8. Hawthorne, *Doubt and Dogma*, 78.

9. James Newcomer, *Maria Edgeworth the Novelist* (Fort Worth, 1967), 56.

10. ME to Mrs. Ruxton, 1809 (?).

11. ME to Mrs. Ruxton, 28 January 1814.

12. ME to J. L. Foster, 28 October 1816.

13. *Quarterly Review* 24 (1821):359.

14. Edgar Rosenberg, *From Shylock to Svengali: Jewish Stereotypes in English Fiction* (Stanford, 1960), 35.

15. Ibid., 52.

16. *Edinburgh Review* 28 (1817):397.

17. Helen Zimmern, *Maria Edgeworth* (London, 1883), 120.

18. Patrick Murray, *Maria Edgeworth: A Study of the Novelist* (Cork, 1971), 63.

19. Elizabeth Eisenstadt, "A Study of Maria Edgeworth's Fiction" (Ph.D. diss., Washington University, 1975), 171.

20. For the development of the "Saintly Jew" in English literature, see Rosenberg, *From Shylock to Svengali,* 39–70.

21. Ibid., 64.

22. *Edinburgh Review* 28 (1817):403.

23. Frank Modder, *The Jew in the Literature of England* (1939; reprint, New York, 1960), 136.

24. ME was no doubt influenced by the tastes of her reading public, as we know from Scott's unwillingness to venture an interfaith marriage in *Ivanhoe.* In Scott's view, "the prejudice of the age rendered such a union almost impossible" (Rosenberg, *From Shylock to Svengali,* 86).

25. *Education of the Heart,* ed. MacDonald, 33.

26. Edgeworth, *Memoir,* 2:287.

27. Modder, *The Jew,* 137.

Chapter Five

1. Maria Edgeworth, *Castle Rackrent,* ed. George Watson (London, 1964), 97; hereafter cited in the text as *CR.*

2. Edgeworth, *Memoir,* 3:253.

3. Ibid., 3:87.

4. Thomas Flanagan, *The Irish Novelists, 1800–1850* (New York, 1958), 38.

5. Butler, *Maria Edgeworth,* 359.

6. Ibid.

7. ME's chief source of anxiety was that Thady's account of the Rackrent landlords would be interpreted as an up-to-date picture of the Irish gentry in 1800. See ibid., 359–60.

8. Horatio Sheafe Krans, *Irish Life in Irish Fiction* (1903; reprint, New York, 1966), 144–45.

9. Newcomer, *Maria Edgeworth,* 144 ff.

10. Stanley J. Solomon, "Ironic Perspective in Maria Edgeworth's *Castle Rackrent," Journal of Narrative Technique* 2 (1972):68.

11. Walter Scott, *The Lives of the Novelists,* Everyman ed. (New York, 1910), 376.

12. Flanagan, *Irish Novelists,* 68.

13. Joanne Altieri, "Style and Purpose in Maria Edgeworth's Fiction," Nineteenth Century Fiction 23 (1968):275. In reference to the Irish, italics nearly always serve a pedagogical function, to call attention to uniquenesses of language or manners. In reference to the English, italics, more often than not, are used to express a negative attitude. In the preface to *Rackrent,* for instance, ME alludes to the *"ignorant* English reader" (4).

14. Gerry H. Brookes, "The Didacticism of Edgeworth's *Castle Rackrent," Studies in English Literature, 1500–1900* 17 (Autumn 1977):598–99.

15. For the "miscellany of real-life events and information" that forms the source material for *Castle Rackrent,* see Butler, *Maria Edgeworth,* 306. The notes and glossary in *Castle Rackrent* are designed to explain (for the English reader) the customs, dialect, and living conditions of the peasantry that Thady represents. The landlord practices of the Rackrent squires (especially Murtagh and Kit) are partially factual accounts heightened for the purpose of fiction. ME wrote to her friend, Mrs. Stark: "As far as I have heard, the characters in 'Castle Rackrent' were, in their day, considered as better classes of Irish characters than any I ever drew" (*Memoir,* 3:153).

16. Altieri, "Style and Purpose in Maria Edgeworth's Fiction," 266.

17. Review of *The Stranger in Ireland; or, A Tour in the Southern and Western Parts of that Country in the Year 1805,* by John Carr, *Edinburgh Review* 10 (1807):59. The review was coauthored by ME and her father and published anonymously.

18. George Watson, introduction to *Castle Rackrent,* xx.

19. Mary Leadbeater, *Cottage Dialogues Among the Irish Peasantry,* with notes and preface by Maria Edgeworth (London, 1811), 333.

20. Ibid., 337.

21. Ibid., 286.

22. Ibid., 337.

23. Ibid., 270.

24. Ibid., 338.

25. Frank O'Connor, *A Short History of Irish Literature* (New York, 1967), 127.

26. Flanagan, *Irish Novelists,* 78.

27. Edgeworth, *Memoir,* 2:298.

28. Flanagan, *Irish Novelists,* 69.

29. The plot is undeniably a unified and coherent whole, but the unity depends primarily on the character of Thady Quirk. The obvious and sustained contrast between the story he tells and his understanding of it has generally been interpreted as irony. Yet much of the irony is inherent in the ambivalencies of Irish character itself. Thady can profitably be compared with the female speaker in "Langan's Defeat," a remarkable little sketch from the family commonplace books (see bibliography). Langan, the boxer, has lost a match on which the speaker has bet heavily. The sketch is her denunciation of him, a revelation of character and personality that says more than volumes.

30. The attitude is evident throughout the nonfictional works alluded to in this chapter. The message that underlies the Irish fiction is less a stance for reliance on the British connection than a plea for equality.

31. Historians of the novel and critics of ME's fiction generally support these conclusions. But see E. A. Baker, *The History of the English Novel,* vol. 6 (London, 1935), 32; Newby, *Maria Edgeworth,* 39; and Watson, introduction to *Castle Rackrent,* xvi ff.

32. In his postscript to *Waverly,* Scott directly acknowledged ME's influence. Cooper and Turgenev no doubt profited from her example although direct influence is more difficult to establish. For similarities among ME, Scott, and Turgenev, see Donald Davie, *The Heyday of Sir Walter Scott* (London, 1961), 66 ff.

33. Butler suggests that "it helped to inaugurate a new style of sociological realism" and that in it "the life of the landlord is realized in fiction for the first time." See *Maria Edgeworth,* 365, 373.

34. Review of *Tales of Fashionable Life* (first series), *Edinburgh Review* 14 (1809):383.

35. Ibid., 385. In the *Quarterly Review* 2 (1809):149 ff., Henry Stephen also stated a decided preference for *Ennui.*

36. Review of *Tales of Fashionable Life* (first series), *British Critic* 34 (1809):73.

37. *Edinburgh Review* 14 (1809):383.

38. ME to Mrs. Ruxton, 21 November 1811.

39. ME to Sophy Ruxton, 22 June 1812; note appended by Mrs. F. E. Edgeworth.

40. Ronald Paulson, *Satire and the Novel in Eighteenth-Century England* (New Haven, 1967), 139.

41. Flanagan, *Irish Novelists,* 89.

42. Sir G. O. Trevelyan, *Life and Letters of Macaulay* (New York, 1875), 2:206.

43. ME to Sneyd and Harriette Edgeworth, 7 May 1817.

44. ME to Harriette Edgeworth, 8 May 1817. ME adds that she "had formed the whole plan & had written two sketches of it above a year ago."

45. Norman Jeffares, "Maria Edgeworth's *Ormond*," *English* 18 (Autumn 1969):87. Throughout the fashionable tales ME shows the harmful influence of reading sentimental novels. In *Ormond*, the hero strikes a balance between Richardson and Fielding and thus creates his own model.

46. Honora Edgeworth to ME, 8 July 1817.

47. Butler, *Maria Edgeworth*, 387–88.

48. Emily Lawless, *Maria Edgeworth* (London, 1904), 143.

49. Quoted in R. J. McHugh, "Maria Edgeworth's Irish Novels," *Studies* 27 (1938):569.

Chapter Six

1. Newby, *Maria Edgeworth*, 93–94.

2. Desmond Clark, *The Ingenious Mr. Edgeworth* (London, 1965), 167.

3. G. E. Hodgson, *Rationalist English Educators*, 144; cited in *The Ingenious Mr. Edgeworth*, 167. The opinion is shared by Alice Paterson in *The Edgeworths*, vi.

4. *Memoirs of Mrs. Inchbald*, ed. James Boaden (London, 1833), 2:195.

5. Baker, *The History of the English Novel*, 6:26.

6. Vineta Colby, *Yesterday's Woman: Domestic Realism in the English Novel* (Princeton, 1974), 97–98.

7. Luisa-Teresa Unthank, "Essence of Common Sense, a Comparative Study of Some of Maria Edgeworth's Fiction for Children" (Ph.D. diss., University of Liverpool, 1973), 282.

8. Butler, *Jane Austen*, 126.

9. Ibid., 130.

10. J. G. Lockhart, *Memoirs of the Life of Sir Walter Scott* (London, 1914), 4:295.

11. Butler, *Maria Edgeworth*, 335.

12. Watson, introduction to *Castle Rackrent*, x.

13. Sir Walter Scott to Joanna Baillie, 11 July 1823; quoted in R. F. Butler, "Maria Edgeworth and Sir Walter Scott: Unpublished Letters, 1823," *Review of English Studies* 9 (1958):25.

14. Allen, *The English Novel*, 416.

15. "Novels Descriptive of Irish Life," *Edinburgh Review* 42 (1831):411–12.

16. Watson, introduction to *Castle Rackrent*, xx.

17. For similarities between *Castle Rackrent* and *The Memoirs of Barry Lyndon*, and ME's possible influence on Thackeray, see Joseph F. Connelly, "Transparent Poses: *Castle Rackrent* and *The Memoirs of Barry Lyndon*," *Eire-Ireland* 14 (Summer 1979):37–43.

18. Butler, *Maria Edgeworth,* 357.

19. Quoted in Grace Oliver, *A Study of Maria Edgeworth With Notices of Her Father and Friends* (Boston, 1882), 508.

20. Quoted in Margaret E. Spence, "Ruskin's Correspondence With Miss Blanche Atkinson," *Bulletin of the John Rylands Library* 42 (September 1959):206.

Selected Bibliography

PRIMARY SOURCES

1. Collected Editions

There are numerous collected editions of ME's *Tales and Novels*. The ten-volume Longford Edition (London: George Routledge & Sons, 1893) is the most accessible. It was reprinted in 1967 (New York: AMS Reprint Series) and in 1969 (Hildesheim: Georg Olms Verlagsbuchhandlung). It includes the tales and novels, but excludes the children's stories, educational works, and fugitive pieces.

2. Published Works

The following list contains the complete published works of ME, arranged chronologically within genre by date of original publication.

a. Fiction and Drama for Adults

Letters for Literary Ladies, to which is added an Essay on the Noble Science of Self-justification. London: J. Johnson, 1795.

Castle Rackrent, an Hibernian tale: taken from the facts, and from the manners of the Irish squires, before the year 1782. London: J. Johnson, 1800. Reprint. London: Oxford University Press, 1964.

Moral Tales for Young People. 5 vols. London: J. Johnson, 1801.

Belinda. 3 vols. London: J. Johnson, 1801.

Popular Tales. 3 vols. London: J. Johnson, 1804.

The Modern Griselda: a tale. London: J. Johnson, 1805.

Leonora. 2 vols. London: J. Johnson, 1806.

Tales of Fashionable Life (Ennui, Almeria, Madame de Fleury, The Dunn, Manoeuvring). London: J. Johnson, 1809.

Tales of Fashionable Life (Vivian, Emilie de Coulanges, The Absentee). London: J. Johnson, 1812.

Patronage. 4 vols. London: R. Hunter, 1814.

Comic Dramas in Three Acts (Love and Law; The Two Guardians; The Rose, the Thistle and the Shamrock). London: R. Hunter, 1817.

Harrington, a Tale; and Ormond, a Tale. 3 vols. London: R. Hunter, 1817.

Helen, a Tale. 3 vols. London: R. Bentley, 1834.

Orlandino. Edinburgh: W. and R. Chambers, 1848.

b. Fiction and Drama for Children
The Parent's Assistant: or Stories for Children. 3 vols. London: J. Johnson,
  1796. 6 vols., 1800.
Early Lessons. London: J. Johnson, 1801–2. *Harry and Lucy,* pts. 1–2, 1801;
  Rosamond, pts. 1–3, 1801; *Frank,* pts. 1–4, 1801; tenth volume, other
  stories, 1801–2.
"The Mental Thermometer." In *The Juvenile Library.* London: T. Hurst,
  1801.
"Little Dominick." In *Wild Roses; or Cottage Tales.* London, 1807.
Continuation of Early Lessons (Harry and Lucy, Frank, Rosamond). 2 vols. Lon-
  don: J. Johnson, 1814.
Rosamond: A Sequel to Early Lessons. 2 vols. London: R. Hunter, 1821.
Frank: A Sequel To Frank in Early Lessons. 3 vols. London: R. Hunter, 1822.
Harry and Lucy Concluded: Being the Last Part of Early Lessons. 4 vols. London:
  R. Hunter, 1825.
*Little Plays for Children (The Grinding Organ, Dumb Andy, The Dame School
  Holiday).* London: R. Hunter, 1827.
Garry-Owen: or the Snow-woman. In *Christmas Box,* 1829; reprinted with *Poor
  Bob the Chimney-sweeper,* 1832.
*The Most Unfortunate Day of My Life: being a hitherto unpublished story, together
  with The Purple Jar and other stories.* London: Cobden-Sanderson, 1931.

c. Treatises on Education
Practical Education. 2 vols. London: J. Johnson, 1798. With RLE. 3 vols.,
  1801 (as *Essays on Practical Education*).
Essays on Professional Education. London: J. Johnson, 1809. By R. L. (and
  Maria) Edgeworth.

d. Autobiography/Biography
*Memoirs of Richard Lovell Edgeworth, Esq.; Begun by Himself and Concluded by
  His Daughter, Maria Edgeworth.* 2 vols. London: R. Hunter, 1820. Re-
  print. Shannon: Irish University Press, 1968. Vol. 1 by RLE; vol. 2 by
  ME.

e. Miscellaneous Writings
Essay on Irish Bulls. London: J. Johnson, 1802. With RLE.
Review of *The Stranger in Ireland; or, a Tour in the Southern and Western Parts
  of that Country in the Year 1805,* by John Carr. *Edinburgh Review* 10
  (1807):40–60. Anonymous review of Carr's travelogue by ME and
  RLE.
*Cottage Dialogues Among the Irish Peasantry, with notes and a Preface by Maria
  Edgeworth.* London: J. Johnson, 1811.

"On French Oaths." In *Irish Farmers Journal* 3 (1815). Published anonymously.
Readings on Poetry. London: R. Hunter, 1816. Preface and last chapter by ME.
"Thoughts on Bores." In *Janus; or the Edinburgh Almanack.* Edinburgh: Oliver and Boyd, 1826. Essay.
"Langan's Defeat" and "An Irish Wedding." Two extracts from surviving family commonplace books. See Christina Colvin, "Two Unpublished MSS. by Maria Edgeworth," *Review of English Literature* 8 (1967):53–61.

3. Published Letters

Butler, Harold E., and Butler, Jessie H. *The Black Book of Edgeworthstown, 1585–1817.* London: Faber & Gwyer, 1927. Invaluable account of Edgeworth family history from late sixteenth through early nineteenth century. Includes family letters.

Butler, R. F. "Maria Edgeworth and Sir Walter Scott: Unpublished Letters, 1823." *Review of English Studies* 9 (1958):23–40. Eleven letters tell story of ME's visit with Scott in 1823.

Colvin, Christina. "Maria Edgeworth's Tours in Ireland: I. Rostrevor." *Studia Neophilologica* 42 (1970):319–29. Two of ME's letters describe her journey to Rostrevor in 1806. Glenthorn's return to his Irish castle in *Ennui* (1809) may be based on ME's description in these letters.

———, ed. *Maria Edgeworth, Letters from England, 1813–1844.* Oxford: Clarendon Press, 1971. An essential collection that contains over a hundred letters not previously printed; provides full context for many previously printed. Generous selection and scrupulous editing.

———, ed. *Maria Edgeworth in France and Switzerland: Selections from the Edgeworth Family Letters.* Oxford: Clarendon Press, 1979. Describes family visits to the Continent in 1802–3 and 1820. Over half the letters not published before. Meticulous editing.

Grey, Rowland. "Maria Edgeworth and Etienne Dumont." *Dublin Review* 145 (1909):239–65. Explores personal relationship between ME and Dumont. Excerpts from letters, 1805–23.

Hare, Augustus J. C., ed. *The Life and Letters of Maria Edgeworth.* 2 vols. London: Edward Arnold, 1894. Long considered the standard edition because of availability. Based on *Memoir* and not family manuscripts.

Häusermann, Hans W. *The Genevese Background.* London: Routledge & Kegan Paul, 1952. Thirty-page introduction provides stimulating if not controversial discussion of ME's debt to the editors of the Bibliothèque Britannique for establishing her continental reputation and of ME's personal and literary relationship with Madame de Stael and Etienne Dumont. Letters from 1801 to 1829.

"Letter of Maria Edgeworth to Mr. Hunter." *Notes and Queries* 12 (June

1923):488. ME outlines her father's judgments of several of her works. Soundness of judgments further supports argument for RLE's competence as critic.

MacDonald, Edgar E., ed. *The Education of the Heart: the Correspondence of Rachel Mordecai Lazarus and Maria Edgeworth.* Chapel Hill: University of North Carolina Press, 1977. Helpful background for *Harrington.* Letters from 1815 to 1838. Carefully researched and edited.

A Memoir of Maria Edgeworth, With a Selection From Her Letters by the late Mrs. [Frances] Edgeworth. Edited by her children. 3 vols. London: Joseph Masters & Son, 1867. Best edition of letters to 1813 although texts are often distorted by family selection and editing.

Oliver, Grace A. *A Study of Maria Edgeworth With Notices of Her Father and Friends.* Boston: A. Williams & Co., 1882. Best researched of older biographies. Narrative amply supported by letters although many are not precisely dated.

4. Manuscripts

Edgeworth-Butler Letters, 1769–1817. National Library of Ireland, Dublin. MSS 10166–67. Several hundred letters from ME and members of her family. Arranged chronologically but not yet catalogued.

SECONDARY SOURCES

1. Bibliographies

Finneran, Richard J., ed. *Anglo-Irish Literature: A Review of Research.* New York: Modern Language Association of America, 1976. The section on nineteenth-century writers, by James F. Kilroy, contains a valuable summary and estimate of Edgeworth scholarship.

Harmon, Maurice. *Select Bibliography for the Study of Anglo-Irish Literature and Its Backgrounds.* Port Credit, Ontario: P. D. Meany, 1977. Helpful guide to major reference works in Anglo-Irish literature.

Slade, Bertha Coolidge. *Maria Edgeworth, 1767–1849: A Bibliographical Tribute.* London: Constable, 1937. Admirable attempt to collate earlier texts. Useful incidental information.

2. Biographies

Butler, Marilyn. *Maria Edgeworth: A Literary Biography.* Oxford: Clarendon Press, 1972. Most modern, most accurately researched, most reliable of all biographies. Detailed bibliography includes major manuscript sources. Sound criticism. Definitive.

Clarke, Desmond. *The Ingenious Mr. Edgeworth.* London: Oldbourne, 1965. The only published biography of ME's father. Clarifies scope of RLE's scientific, educational, and political activities and their importance during his lifetime.

Lawless, Emily. *Maria Edgeworth.* English Men of Letters Series. London: Macmillan & Co., 1904. Useful, but superseded by Butler.

Zimmern, Helen. *Maria Edgeworth.* London: W. H. Allen & Co., 1883. Useful, but superseded by Butler.

3. Criticism and Comment
a. Books

Allen, Walter. *The English Novel.* New York: E. P. Dutton & Co., 1958. Includes brief summary of ME's contributions to the novel.

Arbuthnot, Mary Hill. *Children and Books.* 3d ed. Glenview, Ill.: Scott, Foresman & Co., 1964. Textbook for children's literature courses.

Avery, Gillian. *Childhood's Patterns: A Study of the Heroes and Heroines of Children's Fiction, 1770–1950.* London: Hodder and Stoughton, 1975. Discusses changing tastes in children's literature and the domination of given historical eras by certain types of heroes and heroines.

Baker, E. A. *The History of the English Novel.* Vol. 6, *Edgeworth, Austen, Scott.* 1929. Reprint. London: H. F. & G. Wetherby, 1964. Includes perceptive analysis of ME's fiction.

Bingham, Jane, and Scholt, Grayce. *Fifteen Centuries of Children's Literature: An Annotated Chronology of British and American Works in Historical Context.* Westport, Conn.: Greenwood Press, 1980. An annotated chronological listing of representative books for children from the sixth century to 1945.

Boaden, James, ed. *Memoirs of Mrs. Inchbald.* 2 vols. London: R. Bentley, 1833. Includes letters written by ME and RLE.

Butler, Marilyn. *Jane Austen and the War of Ideas.* Oxford: Clarendon Press, 1975. One chapter on ME shows that she shares traits in common with both Jacobin and anti-Jacobin writers. Compares ME's early fiction with works by her contemporaries and suggests possible influences of ME on Austen.

Byron, George Gordon. "Ravenna Journal." In *Byron's Letters and Journals,* vol. 8, edited by Leslie A. Marchand. Cambridge: Harvard University Press, 1978. Describes impressions of ME and RLE during their London visit in 1813.

Colby, Vineta. *Yesterday's Woman: Domestic Realism in the English Novel.* Princeton: Princeton University Press, 1974. One chapter traces influences of education in fiction by ME and her contemporaries. Helpful historical orientation.

Coley, W. B. "An Early 'Irish' Novelist." In *Minor British Novelists,* edited by Charles A. Hoyt. Carbondale: Southern Illinois Press, 1967. Provides helpful distinctions between the historical novel (as developed by Scott) and the regional novel (as developed by ME). Points out challenging similarities between Faulkner's *The Hamlet* and ME's *Castle Rackrent*.

Cronin, John. *The Anglo-Irish Novel.* Vol. 1, *The Nineteenth Century.* Totowa, N.J.: Barnes & Noble, 1980. One chapter on ME includes a biographical sketch and brief discussion of *Castle Rackrent*.

Darton, F. J. Harvey. "Children's Books." In *Cambridge History of English Literature,* vol. 11, edited by A. W. Ward and A. R. Waller. New York: Macmillan Co., 1917. History and criticism of English children's books from their beginnings through Charles and Mary Lamb.

————. *Children's Books in England.* 1932. Reprint. London: Cambridge University Press, 1960. History and criticism of English children's books in the context of English social life. Best scholarly treatment of children's literature.

Davie, Donald. *The Heyday of Sir Walter Scott.* London: Routledge & Kegan Paul, 1961. One chapter on ME pinpoints similarities of ME, Turgenev, and Scott.

Flanagan, Thomas. *The Irish Novelists, 1800–1850.* New York: Columbia University Press, 1958. While treatment is limited to ME's Irish works, it is perhaps the most able discussion of its kind. Places ME's works within historical context of Ireland's tragic past and views them as evolvements from combined political, historical, and cultural circumstances.

Harden, O. Elizabeth M. *Maria Edgeworth's Art of Prose Fiction.* The Hague: Mouton, 1971. Examines ME's works from modern critical perspective. Surveys all major fiction including children's stories. Argues that artistic blemishes stem mainly from preconceived theses.

Hawthorne, Mark D. *Doubt and Dogma in Maria Edgeworth.* Gainesville: University of Florida Press, 1967. Analyzes thematic structures, interplay of characters, and symbolism to show that ME rejected her father's rationalism until she "incorporated the demands of the passions into his educational theory." Omits several of the major novels although close observations of lesser known works are quite helpful.

Hurst, Michael. *Maria Edgeworth and the Public Scene.* Coral Gables: University of Miami Press, 1969. Uses solid historical approach in attempting "through the life of one highly intelligent and observant woman to pinpoint many of the problems of those times."

Krans, Horatio Sheafe. *Irish Life in Irish Fiction.* 1903. Reprint. New York: AMS Press, 1966. Survey of Irish novel of the first half of the nineteenth century. Observations about ME still useful.

Lockhart, J. G. *Memoirs of Sir Walter Scott.* 5 vols. London: Macmillan &

Co., 1914. Includes correspondence between Scott and ME and details of their mutual visits.

Meigs, Cornelia, et al. *A Critical History of Children's Literature.* New York: Macmillan Co., 1953. Surveys children's books in English from earliest times to the present.

Modder, Frank Montagu. *The Jew in the Literature of England.* 1939. Reprint. Cleveland: World Publishing Co., 1960. Detailed, reliable analysis of the Jew as a character in the literature of England. Helpful background for *Harrington.*

Moore, Annie E. *Literature Old and New for Children: Materials for a College Course.* Cambridge: Houghton Mifflin, 1934. Historical and critical treatment of children's literature.

Murray, Patrick. *Maria Edgeworth: A Study of the Novelist.* Cork: Mercier Press, 1971. Argues that despite major faults—reluctance to grapple seriously with adult issues, exaggerated reliance on contrivance, and oversimplification of experience—many of ME's works still have "valid claims on our attention." Devotes only one chapter to voluminous English works, but offers balanced appraisal of father-daughter partnership.

Newby, Percy Howard. *Maria Edgeworth.* Denver: Alan Swallow, 1950. Succinct and highly readable monograph. Essential as introductory biographical and critical survey. Suggests that "whereas Jane Austen was so much the better novelist Maria Edgeworth may be the more important."

Newcomer, James. *Maria Edgeworth the Novelist.* Fort Worth: Texas Christian University Press, 1967. Opening chapter surveys errors in Edgeworth criticism and shows that neglect has led to misreading and misrepresentation in literary history. Central chapters answer three major charges against ME in this century: "a lack of versimilitude, an overemphasis on morality, and an inability to fashion a plot." Closing chapters view Thady as villain of *Rackrent.* A perceptive, appreciative study of the major fiction.

———. *Maria Edgeworth.* Lewisburg: Bucknell University Press, 1973. Concise biographical and critical survey. Instructive guidebook.

O'Connor, Frank. *A Short History of Irish Literature.* New York: G. P. Putnam's Sons, 1967. Personal interpretation, based upon a series of lectures delivered at Trinity College, Dublin.

Paterson, Alice. *The Edgeworths: A Study of Later Eighteenth Century Education.* London: University Tutorial Press, 1914. Only published study devoted exclusively to the Edgeworths' work in education. Still valuable for summary and analysis of educational treatises and their relationship to the fiction.

Pattison, Robert. *The Child Figure in English Literature.* Athens: University of Georgia Press, 1978. Discusses the conjunction of the child as lit-

erary figure and "two ideas fundamental to Western culture"—the Fall
of Man and Original Sin.

Paulson, Ronald. *Satire and the Novel in Eighteenth-Century England.* New
Haven: Yale University Press, 1967. Discusses "what happened to the
novel when satire entered, and what happened to satire."

Reeve, Clara. *The School for Widows.* 3 vols. London: T. Hookham, 1791.
A didactic novel featuring exemplary female characters.

Rosenberg, Edgar. *From Shylock to Svengali: Jewish Stereotypes in English Fiction.* Stanford: Stanford University Press, 1960. A study of Jewish pro-
totypes, stereotypes, and myths in English fiction. Helpful background
for *Harrington.*

Schofield, Robert E. *The Lunar Society of Birmingham.* Oxford: Clarendon
Press, 1963. Detailed, illuminating study of the men who composed
the Lunar Society and of their contributions which "guided the trans-
formation of England." Helps clarify real significance of RLE's educational, scientific, and political achievements.

Scott, Sir Walter. *The Lives of the Novelists.* Everyman Edition. 1910.
Praises ME's "immortal Thady."

Simon, Brian. *Studies in the History of Education.* London: Lawrence & Wis-
hart, 1960. A study of the growth and development of education in
England. Early chapters are especially helpful to an understanding of
the Edgeworths' work in education.

Tompkins, J. M. S. *The Popular Novel in England, 1770–1800.* Lincoln:
University of Nebraska Press, 1961. Detailed survey of the English
novel and of English reading tastes between 1770 and 1800.

Trevelyan, Sir G. O. *Life and Letters of Macaulay.* 2 vols. in 1. New York:
Harper and Brothers, 1875. Interesting for Macaulay's judgments
about ME's works.

b. Articles

Altieri, Joanne. "Style and Purpose in Maria Edgeworth's Fiction." *Nineteenth Century Fiction* 23 (1968):265–78. Shows how moral and didactic
purposes determine contrasting styles in *Rackrent* and *Absentee* and compares the latter with several popular novels of the period. Informative
and closely reasoned.

Brookes, Gerry H. "The Didacticism of Edgeworth's *Castle Rackrent.*"
Studies in English Literature, 1500–1900 17 (Autumn 1977):593–605.
Argues that *Castle Rackrent* is "implicitly and forcefully didactic" and
views the novel as an apologue shaped from "a thesis about or attitudes
toward the Irish predicament." Response to Harden and Butler, among
others, who see the novel as largely free of didacticism.

Buckley, Mary. "Attitudes to Nationality in Four Nineteenth-Century
Novelists: 1. Maria Edgeworth." *Journal of the Cork Historical and Ar-*

chaeological Society 78 (1973):27–34. Argues Irish nationalist position while admitting that ME used fiction to point out inequalities and injustices of the system.

Butler, Marilyn, and Colvin, Christina. "A Revised Date of Birth for Maria Edgeworth." *Notes and Queries* 18 (1971):339–40. Documentary evidence in ME's own hand and contemporary records indicate that birth date was probably 1 January 1768 rather than 1 January 1767.

Connelly, Joseph F. "Transparent Poses: *Castle Rackrent* and *The Memoirs of Barry Lyndon.*" *Eire-Ireland* 14 (Summer 1979):37–43. Similarities in narrative techniques and approaches to humor "suggest the distinct possibility of influence of Edgeworth's work on Thackeray's."

Davie, Donald. "Miss Edgeworth and Miss Austen: *The Absentee.*" *Irish Writing* 29 (1954):50–56. Argues that in *The Absentee* ME attempts to make ethos of a commercial society (enlightened self-interest) work also in a landed society. Question of absenteeism is not really a moral question but a piece of Benthamite calculation. Concludes that Austen's "reason" is superior to ME's because based on Christian principles.

Edwards, Duane. "The Narrator of *Castle Rackrent.*" *South Atlantic Quarterly* 71 (1972):125–29. A response to Newcomer's reading in *Maria Edgeworth the Novelist*. Maintains that Thady is a more balanced character than Newcomer allows, and yet not the faithful, loyal retainer of traditional interpretations.

Hawthorne, Mark D. "Maria Edgeworth's Unpleasant Lesson: The Shaping of Character." *Studies* 64 (Summer 1975):167–77. Argues that ME's extensive revisions of *Belinda* improved the work by increasing focus on major characters and placing secondary emphasis on the "lesson."

Howard, William. "Regional Perspective in Early Nineteenth-Century Fiction: The Case of *Ormond.*" *Wordsworth Circle* 10 (Autumn 1979):331–38. ME's narrative techniques in *Ormond* enable her to present "realistically the opinions and attitudes of the native Irish without either approving of them or trying to pass them off as her own." Concludes that *Ormond* is ME's best novel.

"Humours and Moralities." *Times Literary Supplement,* 20 May 1949, 328. Argues that *Helen* is the most modern and most readable of ME's novels.

Jeffares, A. Norman. "Maria Edgeworth's *Ormond.*" *English* 18 (Autumn 1969):85–90. Useful summary and criticism of ME's Irish novels in historical context, with special attention to *Ormond*. Notes that achievement in *Ormond* can well be compared to that in *Tom Jones*.

Jeffrey, Francis. Review of *Harrington, a Tale* and *Ormond, a Tale. Edinburgh Review* 28 (1817):390–418. Lengthy discussion of ME's strengths and weaknesses as a writer. Negative view of *Harrington;* positive view of *Ormond.*

————. Review of *Popular Tales*. *Edinburgh Review* 4 (1804):329–37. Favorable review in context of ME's purpose.

————. Review of *Tales of Fashionable Life* (first series). *Edinburgh Review* 14 (1809):375–83. The tales "are actually as perfect as it was possible to make them with safety to the great object of the author."

Kennedy, Sister Eileen. "Genesis of a Fiction: The Edgeworth-Turgenev Relationship." *English Language Notes* 6 (June 1969):271–73. Maintains that Turgenev's indebtedness to ME is probably a fiction.

McHugh, Roger. "Maria Edgeworth's Irish Novels." *Studies* 27 (1938):556–70. Examines conflicting critical positions of those who praise ME for realistic portrayals of Irish life and manners and those who condemn her as an Ascendancy writer, alienated by birth and class from the Irish peasantry. Real truth lies somewhere in between. ME was clearly sympathetic to the Irish and used the " 'national' element in the novel in a better way than her predecessors."

Millhauser, Milton. "Maria Edgeworth as a Social Novelist." *Notes and Queries* 175 (September 1938):204–5. Economic message of *The Absentee* dictates development of the story, basic to a plot that hinges on specific sociological issues. ME is the one major novelist before the Victorians for whom an economic problem could outweigh a romance and thus the first to develop an economic connection between the individual and society. Persuasive thesis much more fully developed in Butler's *Maria Edgeworth*.

"Modern Novels." *Quarterly Review* 24 (1821):352–76. Outlines major flaws of ME's fiction.

Murray, Patrick. "Maria Edgeworth and Her Father: The Literary Partnership." *Eire* 6 (1971):39–50. Balanced appraisal of father-daughter collaboration. RLE's greatest contributions are influences of example and ideas, repeatedly reflected in ME's fiction.

Newby, Percy Howard. "The Achievement of Maria Edgeworth." *Listener*, 9 June 1949, 986–87. Points out ME's achievements in children's literature, regional fiction, and the novel of manners.

"Novels Descriptive of Irish Life." *Edinburgh Review* 42 (1831):410–31. Praises ME's successful delineation of Irish character and manners.

Review of *Tales of Fashionable Life* (first series). *British Critic* 34 (1809):73–74. States decided preference for *Ennui*.

Solomon, Stanley J. "Ironic Perspective in Maria Edgeworth's *Castle Rackrent*." *Journal of Narrative Technique* 2 (1972):68–73. *Castle Rackrent* differs from preceding novels with first-person narration by featuring an unreliable narrator who is also major participant. Ironic perspective thus "works against the reader's ability to establish normative values for the author's point of view."

Spence, Margaret E. "Ruskin's Correspondence With Miss Blanche Atkinson." *Bulletin of the John Rylands Library* 42 (September 1959):194–219. Ruskin praises ME's works as "eternal and classic literature."

Stephen, H. J., and Gifford, W. Review of *Tales of Fashionable Life* (first series). *Quarterly Review* 2 (1809):146–54. Favorable judgments of *Ennui*. Generally unfavorable judgments of other tales.

c. Dissertations

Eisenstadt, Elizabeth R. "A Study of Maria Edgeworth's Fiction." Ph.D. dissertation, Washington University, 1975. Provides a detailed description of a "typical Edgeworthian tale" and assesses value of ME's fiction in its historical and present-day context. Well-researched scholarship.

Unthank, Luisa-Teresa B. "Essence of Common Sense, A Comparative Study of Some of Maria Edgeworth's Fiction for Children." Ph.D. dissertation, University of Liverpool, 1973. Examines influences on ME's success as children's author; compares ME's works with those of predecessors and contemporaries; evaluates ME's contributions to children's literature. Sound judgments.

Index

DATE DUE